All you need to know about
Excel 5.0 for Windows

All you need to know about
Excel 5.0 for Windows

Stephen Copestake

Future Publishing Limited
Beauford Court
30 Monmouth Street
Bath
Avon
BA1 2BW

Future Publishing Limited
Beauford Court
30 Monmouth Street
Bath
Avon
BA1 2BW

ISBN   1 85870 057 4

British Library Cataloguing in Publication Data

A CIP catalogue record for this book is available from the British Library

Books Editor Ian Jones

Cover Design by M4 Marketing Communications Ltd, Newbury, Berkshire
Design and layout by Geoff Oakshott, Ashburton, Devon
Printed and bound by Redwood, Trowbridge, Wiltshire

About the Author

Stephen Copestake is the author of numerous computer software manuals and writes regular column inches for news-stand computer magazines.

He is also a novelist and editor of a long-standing short story magazine.

Dedication

To Rita, for everything.

Introduction

'All You Need to Know about *Excel 5.0 for Windows*' is a practical aid to getting to grips with the basic functions of the program.

The emphasis is on practicality allied to an appreciation of the most useful *Excel* features. There are two key elements which help with this.

Icons and illustrations

The book's text is sprinkled liberally with icons which draw your attention to particularly important or relevant information. Use these as 'flags'. The second element is the presence of plenty of illustrations providing visual explanations of key procedures. With the icons and illustrations, you're led by the hand to a comprehensive knowledge of the basic features in the shortest possible time.

USEFUL TIP

A generally useful piece of information. Any time you see the symbol it will be pointing at a less obvious, but perhaps more effective way of achieving your ends. Or it might offer to take you a step further. You can accept or ignore the advice. In any event, it will still be there if you need it later.

WHAT DOES IT MEAN

This shows you the way through the dense thickets of jargon you might meet in some 'instruction manuals' explaining the whys and wherefores as you go. Technical jargon can be irritating when you don't understand it, but it does save time when you can abbreviate half a dozen or more words into a single expression.

Most programs will offer you a quick way round many routine procedures. For example, the 'long' way of saving your work is to click on the File menu and from there select Save; many software houses have adopted Ctrl+S as the quick way. All you do is hold down the Control Key (marked Ctrl) and type S.

You've just learnt something really valuable! A typical 'don't forget' is to save your work often: every five minutes is a good idea. If you just typed a brilliant letter, capturing every nuance in exquisite prose, you don't want it all to disappear when somebody pulls your plug out of the socket to do a bit of hoovering.

Something to be avoided. It could lead to your having to do some of your work over again. A typical example might be the warning not to fiddle with the set-up of your computer by, say, changing the selected printer or the screen driver.

There are certain things which you should not attempt unless completely sure of what you're doing. If you ignore this advice you won't damage your computer hardware, but you might upset the system temporarily. It would be a good idea to ask someone to help you over this stage.

This is where you find out how easy it can be if you take things one step at a time. You will be sitting in front of your computer with the book open, using the keyboard and the mouse. You'll find out what to do and why you do it. If this is the first time you've used a computer you will also discover that it won't explode if you make a mistake!

Getting the best out of *Excel*

The main program components are covered here. These are all procedures which are essential to get the best out of the program, but they're not the most advanced features. When you're ready to tackle these (for example, macros and *Excel*'s programming language, *Visual Basic* for Applications), you'll need to move on to another book. Additionally, 'All You Need to Know about *Excel 5.0 for Windows*' does not claim to provide instruction on accounting procedures and practices. That has to be an entirely separate area.

Microsoft *Windows*

Having said this, the book does assume a basic familiarity with the Microsoft *Windows* operating system. If you don't have this, you need to buy and use a book on *Windows* before using this text.

Conventions

The conventions have been kept to a minimum. Quite simply, whenever you see a pair of square brackets - [] - surrounding text, you'll know that they're there to emphasise something. Usually, they'll be referring you to an Excel menu, feature or dialogue. For instance, if I ask you to choose the Sort option from the *Excel* Data menu, I'll say something like:

Pull down the [Data] menu and select [Sort].

Sometimes, the square brackets emphasise cell values (numeric or textual). However, they never need to be typed in. For instance, if I ask you to type an entry into a cell, I'll say something like:

Enter [125.95] in E40.

All you have to insert is 125.95 in cell E40.

And that's all there is to it. Have fun using *Excel 5.0 for Windows*!

Clip art

Chapter 11 uses a graphic image to illustrate the use of graphics in *Excel 5.0 for Windows*. Readers might like to know that the image used comes from the Presentation Task Force CGM 4.0 clip art collection

Introduction

Icons and illustrations vi

Getting the best out of *Excel* viii

Chapter 1

Installation and new features 1

Installation 3

What's new in *Excel 5.0 for Windows* 8

Chapter 2

Microsoft *Windows* basics 13

Generic screen components 24

Dialogues 26

Chapter 3

Running *Excel 5.0* for the first time .29

Starting *Excel* 31

Screen components 33

Workbook 35

Worksheets 37

Chapter 4

Setting up a worksheet 45

Creating a new worksheet 47

Moving through worksheets 48

Creating a sample worksheet 57

Chapter 5
Editing & refining worksheets

Editing & refining worksheets 65

Developing the worksheet 67
Deleting worksheet elements 73
Using Format Painter 77
Selection procedures 79

Chapter 6
Advanced worksheets

Advanced worksheets 89

Advanced formatting 91
Advanced cell formatting 95
Gridlines 102
Checking spelling 103
Workspaces 106

Chapter 7
Organising worksheets

Organising worksheets 109

Names 111
Outlining 115
Undo and Repeat 120
Cell notes 122
Hiding data 124

Chapter 8
Printing

Printing 133

Print preview 135
Printing 140
Page Setup 141

Chapter 9
More on functions

More on functions 149
Functions 151
Using Function Wizard 152
Inserting functions directly 155
Arrays 156
Series 160
Using the Fill handle 164
Trends 166
Links 167

Chapter 10
Styles & filter/sort operations

Styles & filter/sort operations 173
Styles 175
'What-if' tables 179
Lists 184
Sort operations 197

Chapter 11
Graphics and charts

Graphics and charts 201
Graphics images 203
Other ways to insert pictures 207
Charts 208
Printing charts 218

Chapter 12

Customising *Excel*

Customising *Excel* 221
Toolbars 223
TipWizard 228
General Preferences 230
Info Window 234
Using Find and Replace 236

Chapter 13

Reports and summaries

Reports and summaries 239
Reports 241
Printing out a report 249
More Wizards 250
Miscellaneous topics 259
TextWizard 262

Index

Index 267

Installation and new features

Raring to go? Here's how to install *Excel* first. Choose the type of installation you need, and then preview *Excel's* new features.

Installation and new features

In this chapter, we look at:

- How to install *Excel 5.0 for Windows*
- New features in version 5.0

Installation

First things first. Before you can use *Excel 5.0 for Windows*, you need to install it onto your hard disk.

Before you start

The following are necessary in order to run *Excel*:

- An IBM compatible 286 (or higher) PC
- A hard disk with at least 23 megabytes of available space for a full installation
- One floppy 3½ inch (or 5¼ inch) drive
- At least 4 megabytes of RAM (preferably more)

RAM

RAM is an acronym for Random Access Memory. Often known as Read/Write memory, RAM is the PC's principal dynamic memory. Here, program instructions are stockpiled and acted on as required. Any information stored in RAM is lost when the PC is switched off.

- Version 3.1 or later of DOS, together with Microsoft *Windows* 3.1 or later.

Additionally, while use of a mouse isn't strictly essential, it is highly recommended. Using a mouse makes many operations easier to perform, and there are some features (for instance, power bars) which can't be accessed without it.

Excel 5.0 for Windows is supplied on nine high-density 3½ inch disks. This means that you have to have a high-density drive to read the disks. However, the process of installation is easy, and reasonably quick. Here's how to go about it.

Backing up

Before you install any program, you should always backup (copy) the program disks first. This procedure protects you against the unlikely event of any of the original disks becoming damaged.

To copy the original *Excel* installation disks, insert the first into the floppy drive (normally A:). Type the following at the DOS prompt and follow the on-screen instructions:

DISKCOPY A: A:

If your floppy drive is designated [B]:, substitute this.

Start Microsoft *Windows* in standard or enhanced mode in the normal way (most users do this by typing [WIN] at the DOS prompt). Insert the disk labelled 'Disk 1 - Setup' into the floppy drive. This is normally entitled A (if yours is called B, use this instead). Now pull down the [File] menu from the [Program Manager] overhead menu bar and select [Run].

In the [Run] dialogue, insert the letter of the disk drive you are using, followed by the Setup command:

A: \ SETUP or **B: \ SETUP** as appropriate

Click on [OK].

Excel's Installation routine now supplies a warning about the advisability of not having other programs running at the same time. If you need to close down any programs, type [Ctrl]-[Esc]. This invokes the [Task List] dialogue. Highlight each program you want to close and click on [End Task].

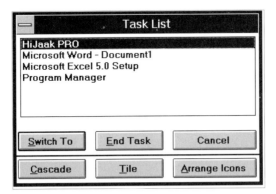

Excel supplies your Product Identification Number (serial no.) here. Make a note of this; you'll need it if you have any queries for Microsoft.

The Installer now needs to know where you want to install *Excel 5.0 for Windows*.

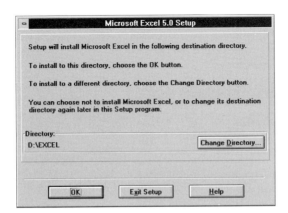

In this instance it has suggested that you install on to Drive D. It has also assumed that the directory which

will hold *Excel 5.0 for Windows* should be entitled
EXCEL, which seems appropriate enough. However, if
you want to install to a different directory and/or to a
different drive, click on [Change Directory].

To amend the installation drive and/or directory, click
with the mouse cursor in the [Path] field. Then type in
the correct entry. Click on [OK] when you've finished.
You're now returned to the earlier dialogue with your
amendments incorporated within it. Click on [OK] to
proceed with the installation.

You now have to make a crucial decision. Which *Excel
5.0 for Windows* program components do you want to
install?

Choose [Laptop] if you're installing onto a portable
computer. Choose [Typical] if your computer system is
standard. Choose [Complete/Custom] if you want
precise control over which components are installed, or
if the availability of hard disk space isn't an issue. For
the sake of brevity, and also because this is the option
most users will select, this chapter will concentrate on
the [Complete/Custom] option. The following
illustration shows the next screen in a [Complete/
Custom] installation.

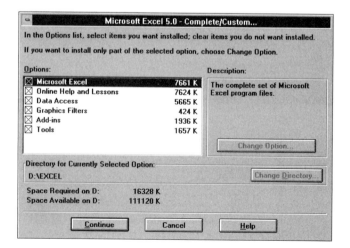

By default, all the available options are selected. If you want every *Excel 5.0 for Windows* component installed, simply click on [Continue]. If you don't need a full installation, click once with the mouse on the unwanted components in the [Options] field.

You can be even more selective than this. For instance, if you only want to install the Graphic Filters you actually need, highlight [Graphic Filters] and click on [Change Option].

 Graphics filters are internal programs which translate graphics images (e.g. clip art) and insert them into *Excel* spreadsheets.

Now follow the on-screen instructions. Click on [Continue] to proceed with the installation.

There is one further decision you have to make: which *Windows* program group do you want the *Excel* program icons installed into?

If you already have other recent Microsoft programs on your system (e.g. *Word 6.0 for Windows*), the Installer offers to insert the *Excel* icons into the existing 'Microsoft Office' group.

If you want this, choose [Continue]. If this isn't convenient, simply highlight one of your existing program groups in the [Existing Groups] field and click on [Continue]. Or type in the name of a new group in the [Program Group] field so that *Excel*'s Installer will create a new one, then click on [Continue] to have the *Excel* icons inserted in this.

You're now ready to run *Excel*. See Chapter 3 for more information.

What's new in *Excel 5.0 for Windows*

For those of you who've used earlier versions of *Excel for Windows*, here are brief details of the main enhancements:

- Greatly increased ease of use (e.g. IntelliSense and the inclusion of 'wizards')

- A new workbook model

- New worksheet features (new toolbars, for instance the Pivot Table toolbar)

- Charting improvements

- Format Painter

- OLE 2.0

Ease of use

The enhanced ease of use is perhaps the most beneficial, both for beginners and people already proficient. *Excel 5.0 for Windows* incorporates IntelliSense.

IntelliSense

IntelliSense is actually a group of associated features. It sits in the background observing your work in *Excel 5.0 for Windows*. Its aim is to perceive what you're trying to do and to enable you to achieve this more easily and conveniently.

Excel 5 includes several 'wizards'. Wizards talk you through tasks, and generally make them much less daunting. ChartWizard, for example, leads you through the creation of charts for your worksheets by supplying five easy-to-complete dialogue 'steps'. We'll deal with this in more detail in Chapter 11. In the meantime, here's a sample ChartWizard screen.

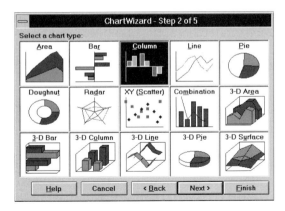

In this screen, ChartWizard is asking you to select the overall chart type. In other screens, you designate axes and specific formats within chart types.

Excel also has TipWizard. TipWizard is especially unique; it monitors your actions. When TipWizard decides that an action you've just performed could have been carried out more rapidly or efficiently, the TipWizard icon in the overhead toolbar 'lights up'. Click on this and a tip appears. Sometimes the tip will supply information related to the task you've just performed. Often, TipWizard produces a copy of the button associated with the task in hand so that you can try it out then and there.

Another example. TextWizard makes importing text files into *Excel* spreadsheets easier. It automatically recognises columnar information and tries to fit the information into cells in a logical and beneficial way.

New workbook model/features

Excel 5.0 for Windows now incorporates the concept of 'workbooks'. Workbooks are collections of interrelated worksheets and charts. As a result of this, *Excel* formulae can be made to apply across worksheets within a workbook, as can range names.

Here's another improvement. The new *Excel*
workbook model incorporates sheet tabs for rapid
access. The tabs appear in a row across the bottom of
the *Excel 5.0 for Windows* screen.

Sheet tabs

To switch to another worksheet, simply click on the
relevant tab. You can also select multiple sheet tabs for
operations on more than one sheet (e.g. deletion). Each
workbook now has 16 worksheets by default (you can
amend this if you want), and new formatting
properties for each worksheet. For more information
on using sheet tabs, see 'Sheet Tabs' in Chapter 3.

Toolbars

There are new toolbars for customising worksheets.
For example, the Tip Wizard has its own toolbar.

Pivot Tables replace the Crosstab Wizard in *Excel 4 for
Windows*. They're much more intuitive: they allow you
to summarise, evaluate and manipulate data in lists
and tables. A Pivot Table Wizard guides you through
the step-by-step creation of the table. For more
information, see 'Pivot Tables' in Chapter 13.

Chart creation

Improvements to chart creation include:

- ChartWizard, which helps with chart creation.

- The ability to apply preset chart types and formats
automatically with the use of the AutoFormat feature.

Format Painter

Format Painter lets you copy formatting information from selected worksheet cells and apply them to others, all with just a few clicks of the mouse.

For more information, see 'Using Format Painter' in Chapter 5.

OLE 2.0

OLE 2.0 provides in-place editing of *Excel* Charts and worksheets which have been inserted as objects into other programs which support OLE 2.0 (for instance, *Word 6.0 for Windows*). The advantage of OLE is that:

1. Any changes you make to a chart in *Excel* are automatically reflected in the destination program (e.g. *Word*), and

2. You can edit the object directly in the destination program.

For more information, see 'OLE Links' in Chapter 11.

In the next chapter, we take a look at some *Windows* basics.

Microsoft *Windows* basics

Before you power-up *Excel*, some brief notes on Microsoft *Windows* and using menus, on-screen windows/toolbars and dialogues. Interested in finding out what *Excel's* screen is like? Read on!

2

Microsoft *Windows* basics

Excel 5.0 runs under Microsoft *Windows 3.0* or *3.1*, which is an easy to use Graphical User Interface (GUI) running on top of the standard operating system, DOS.

As such, you need to have basic *Windows* operating skills in order to use *Excel 5.0*. *Excel 5.0* conforms to standard *Windows* operating techniques.

This chapter offers a brief introduction to the way in which *Excel* implements some of the major examples of these. If you need further information on *Windows* generally, you need to buy and work with a separate text. Alternatively, study the documentation which came with your version of *Windows*.

Using the mouse

Microsoft *Windows* is a GUI environment.

 A GUI, or Graphical User Interface, is a design for that part of an operating system which interacts with the user.

GUIs allow the user to interact with a computer visually, since most people find graphic representations preferable to words or phrases. In a GUI, computer processes are represented by small pictures, or icons. For instance, files, drives, programs and directories can all be represented by icons.

As such, *Excel 5.0* responds best to the use of a mouse. You can use the keyboard, to operate *Excel*, but not as conveniently or easily. Look at the next illustration.

This is the standard Excel opening screen.

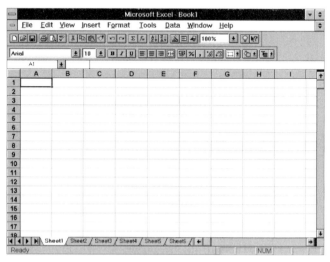

With a mouse, you can very easily initiate any *Excel* operation. Here's an example: to produce a menu, simply click with the left mouse button on an entry in the overhead menu bar. Clicking on [Format], for instance, produces the Format dialogue.

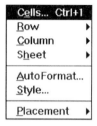

You can use the keyboard to launch an *Excel* menu. Press [Alt] together with the letter underlined in the menu bar. The keyboard route to the Format menu is

[Alt]-[O]. The disadvantage to keyboard routes is that they aren't as easy to use.

You can use the mouse to maximise and minimise windows.

Maximise & minimise windows

Windows are, not unnaturally, central to the use of Microsoft *Windows*. In the context of *Excel 5.0 for Windows*, a window can be defined as an on-screen rectangle providing a representation of worksheets (for information on worksheets, see Chapters 4 to 7). *Excel* windows can be re-sized by the user. When they fill the available editing work area, they're said to be maximised. On the other hand, minimised windows appear as on screen icons.

Maximising and minimising windows

To minimise a window down to an icon, click on the downward pointing arrowhead on the left of the pair in the top right-hand corner of the window.

Excel's minimised icon on the Microsoft Windows Program Manager background.

To convert a minimised icon back to a maximised window, double-click on it with the left mouse button.

Like all true *Windows* applications, *Excel 5.0 for Windows* provides a menu route to maximise and minimise windows. Click on the Control button at the extreme top left of the window to launch the relevant menu. Select [Minimise] or [Maximise], as appropriate.

Zoom

Excel 5.0 for Windows also lets you adjust the size of worksheet windows by increasing window magnification. You can do this in two principal ways. You can use a menu route, or you can use *Excel's* toolbars.

The menu route

Pull down the [View] menu and select [Zoom]. In the [Zoom] dialogue, click on the level of magnification you need.

Fit Selection

Click on [Fit Selection] to calculate a zoom percentage which allows the selected cells or chart sheet to fit in the current window size. For more information on cell selection, see Chapter 5. See Chapter 11 for more information on chart sheets.

If the level of magnification you need isn't listed in the dialogue, click on [Custom] and enter the correct percentage in the text entry field. Click on [OK] to confirm.

The toolbar route

Chapter 3 discusses *Excel's* toolbars in some detail, while Chapter 12 tells you how to customise them.

Formatting toolbar

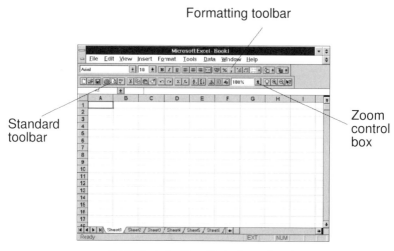

Standard toolbar

Zoom control box

Excel's Standard and Formatting toolbars are flagged.

Toolbars are rows of on-screen icons. The icons represent frequently used commands, and provide the user with very rapid access to the relevant features.

Microsoft *Excel* initiated the use of toolbars some time ago. Now, it provides a wide variety of fully customisable toolbars. You can even create your own.

By default, *Excel 5.0 for Windows* displays the Standard and Formatting toolbars. However, you can control which toolbars appear on screen, and you can incorporate additional icons. See Chapter 12 for further information.

To launch the command associated with a toolbar icon, you simply have to double- click on it with the left mouse button.

To adjust the zoom level, click on the down-pointing arrow to the right of the Zoom control box (see the last illustration). Select the level you need from the list which appears. Or click in the text entry box to the left of the arrow and type in the level you want. Then press ENTER to confirm.

Moving windows

Excel 5.0 for Windows lets you move windows freely (as long as they're not maximised). Again, there are keyboard and mouse routes, although the second is easier.

The keyboard route

Press [Alt]-SPACEBAR to pull down the Control menu. Choose [Move]. The cursor changes to a cross. The next illustration shows a small section of an *Excel* worksheet complete with cross.

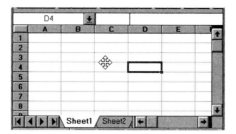

[Move] is unavailable if the window is maximised.

Use the cursor keys to move the *Excel* window to the new location. When you've finished, press ENTER to confirm.

The mouse route

Click on the window's title bar. Hold down the left button and drag the window to the new location. Release the button to confirm. This technique also works with dialogue boxes.

Moving icons

You can also use the mouse to drag minimised icons. Simply click on the icon. Hold down the left button and drag the icon to the new location. Release the button to implement the move.

Closing windows

Once again, there are keyboard and mouse routes, though in this case the keyboard route is arguably more convenient.

The keyboard route

To close the overall *Excel* window, press [Alt]-[F4]; this method forces *Excel 5.0 for Windows* to terminate. To close an individual *Excel* window, press [Ctrl]-[F4].

The mouse route

To close the overall *Excel* window, double-click on the *Excel* Control button. To close an individual *Excel* window, double-click on the window's Control button.

You should get into the habit of saving your worksheet information before you close *Excel* windows.

However, *Excel 5.0 for Windows* provides a fail-safe system to ensure you don't forget to save your work. If you've made changes to an *Excel* window which hasn't been saved, the following message appears when you try to close it:

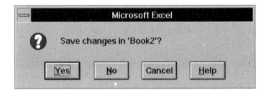

Click on [Yes] to save the changes and then close the window. [No] closes it without saving your work. [Cancel] abandons the closing operation.

Cascading and tiling windows

Excel 5.0 for Windows implements the standard Microsoft *Windows* Cascade and Tile functions.

Cascading

Cascading is the process of displaying multiple windows on screen so that the title bars are all visible. Although the uppermost window occupies most of the screen, the title bars of all the remaining windows display. Cascaded windows give you an excellent overview of available windows while you work in just one. With cascading, the active window always appears on top.

Tiling

Tiling causes the windows to overlap, so that the contents of each are visible. This is the most convenient mode for working with multiple windows.

The next illustrations show cascaded and tiled windows respectively.

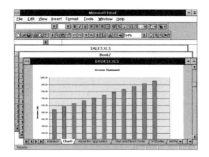 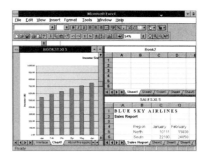

Here's how to cascade and tile windows. Pull down the [Window] menu and choose [Arrange]. In the [Arrange Window] dialogue, select [Tiled] or [Cascade]. Click on [OK].

Moving between windows

Using the keyboard, with either cascaded or tiled windows, press [Ctrl]-TAB to move between open windows. There are mouse techniques, too.

With cascaded windows, click on the title bar of a hidden window to display it. With tiled windows, click anywhere within the window.

Horizontal and vertical windows

Excel 5.0 for Windows has a special implementation of document windows. You can arrange to have windows displayed horizontally or vertically.

Splitting windows

Normally, you can only view an *Excel* worksheet in one window. If you want more than one view of a worksheet, follow this route. Position the editing

cursor at the point within a worksheet where you wish
the split to take effect. Pull down the [Window] menu
and click on [Split].

The result of
splitting a
worksheet.

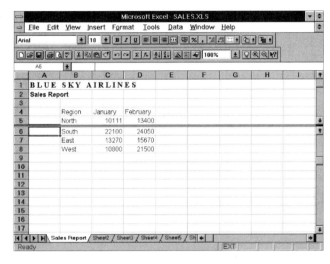

You can use the scroll bar in one half of the split to
move through the worksheet while the view in the
second half is unaltered.

To remove the split-screen effect, pull down the
[Window] menu and select [Remove Split].

Re-sizing windows

Excel 5.0 for Windows implements standard Microsoft
Windows re-sizing techniques. You can use the mouse
to expand or contract windows, or you can use
keyboard techniques.

Using the mouse

Position the mouse cursor over the top, bottom, right or
left page edges of an active window. The cursor
changes into a double-headed arrow.

Click and hold down the left mouse button. Drag the side out to expand the window or in to contract it. Release the button when you've finished.

To re-size a window both horizontally and vertically at once, position the cursor on any window corner and follow the above procedure.

Using the keyboard

Click on the window control button. Choose [Size] from the menu. Note that [Size] is unavailable if the window is currently maximised. Use the cursor keys to re-size the window. Press ENTER when you've finished.

Generic screen components

We'll be looking at *Excel*'s screen in considerable detail in Chapter 3. For the moment, let's examine the way *Excel* implements components which are common to all *Windows* applications. Look at the illustration.

Here we have the Title bar, scroll bars, menu bar and status bar flagged.

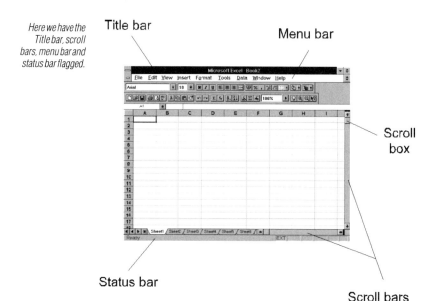

Title bar

The title bar has two main functions in *Excel*.

1. It displays the name of the window/document which you're currently working with.

2. If you have more than one window open at a time, it tells you which one is active.

A window is 'active' when the editing cursor is positioned within it.

Window size

If a window isn't currently displaying full-screen, double-clicking on its title bar maximises it. If it is full-screen, the same procedure shrinks it to the size and location it had before you maximized it.

Scroll bars

Scroll bars are the shaded bars on the right and bottom of a window. With the scroll bars, you can move through a long worksheet. There are several techniques you can use:

1. A very useful component of scroll bars is the scroll box. You can use the position of the box to gauge your progress through a worksheet. To scroll quickly to another part of the worksheet, position the mouse pointer over the box. Click and hold with the left mouse button. Drag the box along the scroll bar to move to the worksheet location you need. Release the mouse button to confirm.

2. To move quickly to the last row used in your worksheet, hold down [Ctrl] while you drag the scroll box to the bottom of the scroll bar.

3. To move one window in a given direction, click the bar on that side of the scroll box.

4. To move one row or column in a given direction, click the arrow at that end of the bar. (For information on rows and columns, see Chapter 3.)

The menu bar

The menu bar is simply a launch pad from which you can invoke *Excel*'s menus and dialogues. You can use both mouse and keyboard techniques to do this.

Using the mouse, click on an entry to pull down the associated menu. Using the keyboard, *Excel* lets you pull down menus by using the [Alt] key with the underlined character in the menu title, for instance, to launch the [File] menu, press [Alt]-[F].

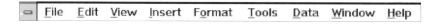

Note that it isn't always the first letter which is underlined, to avoid confusion. For instance, to launch the [Format] menu you press [Alt]-[O], because [Alt]-[F] is already defined.

Dialogues

Selecting an option within an *Excel* menu produces one of the following results:

- A sub-menu
- A dialogue box
- An action is initiated

Excel tells you that a menu entry leads to a sub-menu by placing an arrow to the right of it. Dialogues, on the other hand, are announced by [...]. If neither dots nor arrows are present, selecting the option initiates an action directly.

The next illustration shows the result of clicking on [Row] in the [Format] menu.

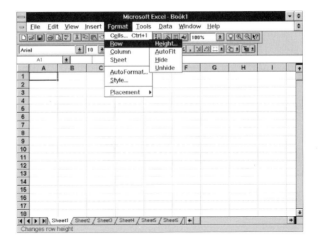

Since there are no arrows next to any of the sub-menu entries, we know that there are no further sub-menus (in any case, *Excel* doesn't nest sub-menus in sub-menus). Since [Height ...] contains dots, we know that selecting it will produce the appropriate dialogue.

Since the other sub-menu options contain neither dots nor arrows, we know that selecting them will initiate the appropriate action directly.

 You can also access many *Excel* menu options through the use of the toolbars. (See Chapter 3 for more information on the use of toolbars.)

3

Running *Excel 5.0* for the first time

At last! Fire up *Windows* and *Excel*. *Excel's* screen components in more detail. What are workbooks and worksheets and how do you use them? It's all here. Columns, rows, cells, the formula bar and sheet tabs explained.

3

Running *Excel 5.0* for the first time

Starting *Excel*

Before you can run *Excel 5.0 for Windows*, you need to start Microsoft *Windows*. Here's how to do both:

1. Start *Windows* in the normal way. For most people, this will mean typing [Win] at the DOS prompt and pressing RETURN.

2. When *Windows* has loaded, launch the *Windows* program group which contains your *Excel* icon by double-clicking on its icon. Unless you chose otherwise during *Excel's* installation, this will be the [Microsoft *Office*] program group.

Your Microsoft Office program group may not look exactly like this.

3. Double-click on the [Microsoft *Excel*] icon.

Keyboard route

You can use a keyboard route to do this. Ensure that the [Microsoft Office] program group is active (if it isn't, press [Ctrl]-TAB until it is). Use the cursor keys to highlight the [Microsoft *Excel*] icon and press ENTER.

Launching *Excel 5.0* automatically

If you use *Excel* frequently, you can arrange for it to launch automatically each time you run *Windows*. Here's how to do this. Follow Step 1 on the previous page to launch Microsoft *Windows*. Then launch your [Microsoft Office] and [Startup] program groups.

Click and hold on the [Microsoft *Excel*] icon. Drag it into the [Startup] program group. Release the mouse button to confirm. Now, each time you run Microsoft *Windows*, *Excel* will also launch without your having to initiate it. The next illustration shows the *Excel* opening screen.

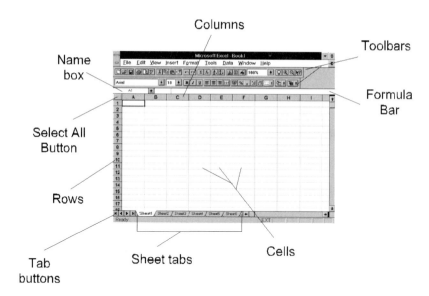

This is part of one worksheet within one workbook (in this case, Book1)

The main *Excel*-specific screen components are flagged. We'll now look at these in some detail. Along the way, we'll discuss some key *Excel* terms and concepts. See Chapter 4 for more detailed information on how to work with most of these screen components.

Screen components

Toolbars

We discussed toolbars in general terms in Chapter 2. Chapter 12 tells you how to customise them to your own specifications. Here, we'll look at their general function, and how to determine which toolbars are currently displayed.

Excel 5.0 comes with a wide selection of pre-defined toolbars. To see what's available, move the mouse pointer over any toolbar currently displayed and right-click once. *Excel 5.0* launches a special 'short-cut' menu.

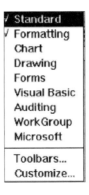

Short-cut menus

Short-cut menus provide rapid and convenient access to common *Excel* menu commands. Most of their features duplicate options available within the standard [Edit] and [Format] menus.

However, some short-cut menus – for instance, the Toolbar short-cut menu – provide access to options which are otherwise unavailable. Short-cut menus are always reached by clicking once with the right mouse button over an item in an *Excel* window.

The short-cut menu doesn't list all available toolbars, only the most common. For access to all toolbars, see 'Accessing Toolbars Through the Keyboard'.

If you want *Excel* to display an additional toolbar, left-click on it in the short-cut menu; a tick appears against it. If a toolbar is currently displayed and you want to hide it, left-click on its entry in the short-cut menu; the tick disappears.

Toolbars through the keyboard

You can also use a menu route to select which toolbars display. Pull down the [View] menu and select [Toolbars].

In the [Toolbars] field in the [Toolbars] dialogue, click on those you want to display; the box to the left is checked. When you've finished, click on [OK].

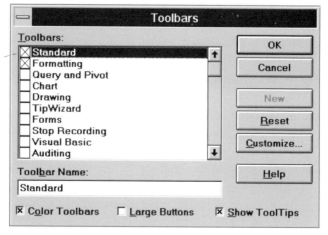

Toolbars

By default, *Excel 5.0 for Windows* displays its [Standard] and [Formatting] toolbars. These provide access to the features most users will use most of the time.

Not all toolbars display along the entire length of the *Excel* screen. Look at the next illustration.

*This shows the
[Chart] toolbar.
(See Chapter 11 for
more information
on Excel's use of
charts.)*

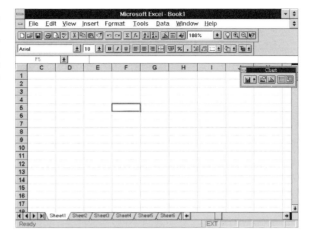

**Function of
buttons**

If you move the mouse pointer over a toolbar button, a
small box appears underneath the button displaying its
name. In addition, *Excel's* status bar carries some brief
explanatory text describing the button's function.

Workbook

Workbooks are the essential *Excel* documents.
Workbooks are modelled on stacks of spreadsheet
paper. They can consist of worksheets (see below) and
charts, in any permutations. Information is entered
into worksheets, and mapped out into Charts (for more
information on charts, see Chapter 11). Charts make
data easier to understand because they're visual.

When you create a new *Excel* document, what you're
actually doing is creating a workbook. Each new
workbook usually has a default name like [Book?],
where the [?] is a number.

Worksheets

Each new workbook comes with 16 worksheets (also
known as 'sheets'), by default. You can change the
number of worksheets for each new workbook; see
Chapter 12 for further information.

Creating a new workbook

Here's how to create a new workbook. Pull down the
[File] menu and choose [New], or click on the [New
Workbook] button on extreme left of the [Standard]
toolbar.

Opening existing workbooks

Pull down the [File] menu and choose [Open].
Alternatively, press [Ctrl]-[O].

In the [Open] dialogue, locate the directory which
holds the workbook in the [Directories] box. If you
need to change drives to do so, click on the down-
pointing arrow to the right of the [Drives] field and
select the new drive from the list which appears. Now
choose the directory. When you've located the correct
directory, associated file names appear in the [File
Name] box; highlight the correct workbook and click on
[OK] to open it.

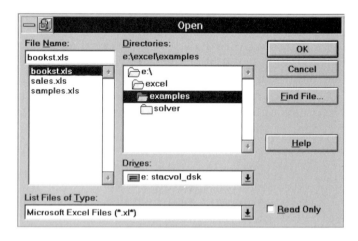

**Opening
workbooks**

Excel 5.0 for Windows stores details of the last four
workbooks you've opened at the base of the [File]
menu. To reopen any of these, pull down the [File]
menu and click on the appropriate entry.

Worksheets

Worksheets are the essential building blocks of workbooks. They consist of rows (horizontal) and columns (vertical), and cells (see below) into which information is entered. This information can be in the form of:

- Descriptive labels (text)
- Values (numbers)
- Mathematical formulae

The beauty of *Excel 5.0 for Windows* is that it can use formulae to return values.

 Let's take an example. If you have a sequence of cells, the final one of which is the total of the preceding ones, the advantage to inserting a formula representing this instead of a specific value is that, if you change any of the earlier cells, the total is automatically updated. Formulae provide automation.

Worksheets can also contain graphics images (see Chapter 11).

 Worksheets can consist of a total of 256 columns and 16,384 rows. This provides 4,194,304 cells, more than enough for any spreadsheet.

Inserting new worksheets

To insert a new worksheet into a workbook, do the following. From within the relevant workbook, pull down the [Insert] menu and select [Worksheet]. Or select [Chart] if you want to add a new chart sheet (see Chapter 11 for more information on charting with *Excel 5.0*).

 You can use a short-cut menu to do this. Right-click on any of the current sheet tabs (see later). The following short-cut menu appears:

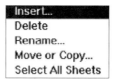

Choose [Insert]. In the [Insert] dialogue, make the appropriate selection and click on [OK].

Refer to Chapters 4, 5, 6 and 7 for detailed information on how to work with worksheets).

Columns, rows and cells

Worksheets are divided into columns and rows.

 Columns are vertical, rows horizontal.

Cell A1 is formed by the intersection of column A with row 1, and so on throughout the worksheet.

Cell addresses Cell addresses are particularly productive in formulae. If you specify a cell address in a formula, *Excel 5.0 for Windows* enters the value stored in the cell into the formula.

There's another component to cell addresses in *Excel 5.0 for Windows*: you can specify the worksheet as well. For instance, the address '4!F86' identifies the cell as being at the intersection of row 86 and column F in worksheet 4.

You can apply a variety of formatting enhancements to rows, columns and cells (see Chapter 4). You can also organise cells into 'ranges'.

A range of cells is a specified rectangle of cells. Look at the next illustration.

Here, a group of cells has been selected in order to perform an Excel operation of some kind on them.

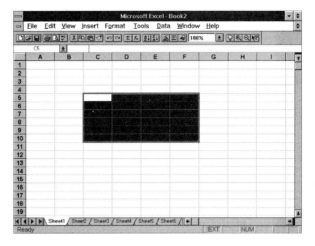

When *Excel 5.0 for Windows* selects groups of cells, it colours them black.

As well as defining individual cells in terms of columns and rows, *Excel 5.0 for Windows* needs to provide a definition for groups of cells. It does this by using the upper left and bottom right cell addresses, separated by a colon. In our example, this would be: C5:F10. *Excel* calls this the 'range address'.

Formula bar

The formula bar reflects the contents of selected cells. Look at the next illustration.

This is a sample workbook entitled SALES.XLS which accompanies Excel. The cursor is currently on cell C5, whose contents are mirrored in the formula bar.

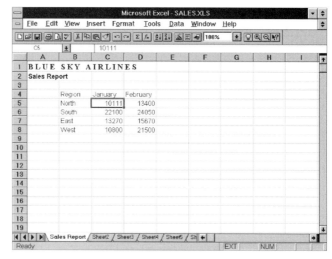

The formula bar displays labels, values and formulae. You can use it to edit cell contents. Simply click in the bar and make any changes you need. When you've finished, press RETURN.

You can also edit cell contents directly, simply by clicking within the relevant cell. See Chapter 4 for more information.

Name box

The name box is a simple and straightforward way to assign names to a cell, or to a range of cells.

The advantage of using names instead of column/row coordinates is that they're easier to recall and use, especially in formulae.

Here's how to use the name box. Click within a cell to select it (or select a cell range). Click inside the name box.

Unless you tell *Excel* otherwise, the name box displays the standard cell reference.

*Enter the name you
want to apply.
Press RETURN
when you've
finished. For more
detailed
information on the
use of names, see
Chapter 7.*

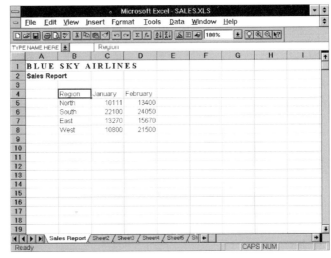

Select All button

Click on this button to select the contents of an entire
worksheet. Pressing [Ctrl]-SHIFT-SPACEBAR
achieves the same result, using the keyboard. You
can't reverse this selection by clicking on the Select All
button. Instead, click within any cell. See Chapter 5
for more information on selecting.

Sheet tabs

These are new to *Excel 5.0*. Sheet tabs are very useful
because you can use them to accomplish a variety of
operations on worksheets.

For instance, click on a sheet tab to make it the active
sheet. The name on the active sheet tab is emboldened.
To scroll through the sheet tabs, use the tab scrolling
buttons to the left of the tabs.

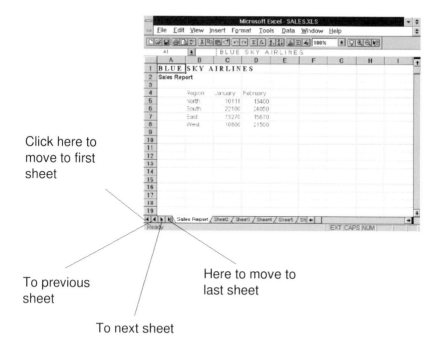

Click here to
move to first
sheet

To previous
sheet

To next sheet

Here to move to
last sheet

There are useful keyboard alternatives here. Press [Ctrl]-[Page Up] to move to the previous worksheet. [Ctrl]-[Page Down] moves to the next worksheet.

Here's a useful technique. You can use sheet tabs to add more sheets to the current workbook (see 'Inserting New Worksheets' earlier for details of an alternative menu route). You do so by copying a specific tab. Here's how to do this.

Hold down the [Ctrl] key and left-click on the sheet tab you want to copy. Hold down the mouse button and drag the tab to the left or right. Release the button to confirm.

The next illustration shows sheet 6 of SALES.XLS. Sheet 6 has been copied; *Excel* automatically names the new sheet [Sheet 6(2)].

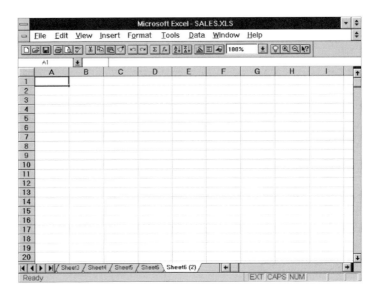

 If you follow this procedure but don't hold down the [Ctrl] key, *Excel* moves the sheet instead.

You can also use sheet tabs to select specific worksheets; see Chapter 5 for more information.

4

Setting up a worksheet

Now you can create your first
worksheet. How do you move
around in it, amend cell contents
and cell/column size? Read on!
Excel can handle very large
numbers – here's how.

Setting up a worksheet

In this chapter, we look at features involved in creating a new worksheet. These include:

- Defining cells
- Moving through the worksheet
- Copying cell contents
- Changing column width and row height
- Entering text

Creating a new worksheet

Start *Excel 5.0 for Windows* in the normal way (see Chapter 3 for how to do this). *Excel* produces its standard opening screen.

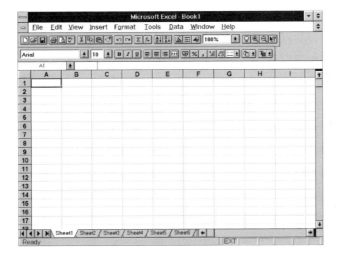

Clean slate

If you want to start with a clean slate, as it were, create a new workbook before you define the worksheet. To do this, pull down the [File] menu and click on [New]. Or press [Ctrl]-[N].

By default, *Excel* allocates 16 worksheets to every new workbook. You therefore have 16 sheets available for immediate use. If you don't want to work with Sheet 1, choose another. You do this by clicking on the appropriate sheet tab at the base of the screen.

Tab scrolling

If the tab for the sheet you want to activate isn't currently visible, use the tab scrolling buttons to the left of the tabs (see Chapter 3 for more information on sheet tabs and scrolling buttons).

Alternatively, press [Ctrl]-[Page Up] or [Ctrl]-[Page Down] to move to the next or preceding sheet, respectively.

Before we start to create our worksheet, we need to discuss the basics of worksheet navigation.

Moving through worksheets

Moving to cells which are visible is easy: simply click in the cell you want to move to. Or use the cursor keys to move to it. This is quite straightforward. However, what happens if you need to move to a cell which you can't see?

Moving to cells which aren't visible – there are several methods which you can use to move to cells (or cell ranges) which are currently off-screen:

- Using the scroll bars
- Using key combinations
- Using Go To

Let's look at these in some detail.

Using scroll bars

Unless you're working with a very large worksheet (in which case, see 'Using Go To', later), scroll bars are often the quickest way for mouse users to move round worksheets (see Chapter 2 for how to use scroll bars).

Using key combinations

Excel provides a variety of keystroke combinations:

1. Use the cursor keys to move to the left, right, up or down.

2. Hold down the [Ctrl] key as you press any of the cursor keys; this jumps to the edge of the current section. For instance, if you press [Ctrl] with the right cursor key while cell A1 is selected, this moves the cursor to cell IV1, the last cell in row 1.

3. Press [Home] to move to the first cell in the current row. For example, if cell F4 is active, [Home] moves you to A4.

4. [Page Up] and [Page Down] move up and down by one screen, respectively.

5. [Alt]-[Page Up] and [Alt]-[Page Down] move one screen to the right and left, respectively.

6. Press [Ctrl]-[Home] from wherever you happen to be in a worksheet to move to the very first cell.

7. [Ctrl]-[End] moves to the lowest cell on the right in active worksheets (relative to the last occupied cell).

Using Go To

Either pull down the [Edit] menu and select [Go To], or press [Ctrl]-[G] or [F5]. The [Go To] dialogue launches.

Enter the coordinates for the cell you want to move to in the [Reference] field. Click on [OK] to confirm.

 If you've defined cell ranges, these are listed in the [Go to] box. To move to a range, highlight it.

To enter information into a cell, you have to select it first (Chapter 5 goes into selection in greater detail).

By default, when you open a new sheet *Excel* selects
cell A1. To distinguish the selected cell from its
neighbours, *Excel 5.0 for Windows* surrounds it with a
frame. See the first illustration in this chapter.

The cell coordinates are displayed in the Name bar.

To select another cell which is visible, simply click in it.
To select a cell which is currently off-screen, use the
techniques discussed in 'Moving to Cells Which Aren't
Visible' earlier.

Entering information

Once a cell has been selected, you can enter
information immediately. What you type appears in
both the cell, and the Formula Bar (see 'Formula Bar'
in Chapter 3.

If you wanted to change the number, you could do so in
the cell itself, but it's often more convenient to work in
the Formula Bar. When you've finished inserting
information into the cell, you can confirm the operation
in two ways:

- **Using the keyboard**
  press RETURN. *Excel* completes the entry and selects
  the next cell down in the current column.

- **Using the mouse**
  click on the [Enter] box.

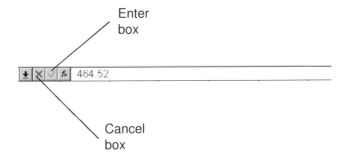

Enter
box

464.52

Cancel
box

If you want to cancel what you've entered into a cell, do
the following.

- **Using the keyboard**
  press [Esc].

- **Using the mouse**
  click on the [Cancel] box.

Following either of these routes empties the cell.

Amending the contents of existing cells

Numbers have been entered into cells B1 to B4. This is expressed in Excel as B1:B4.

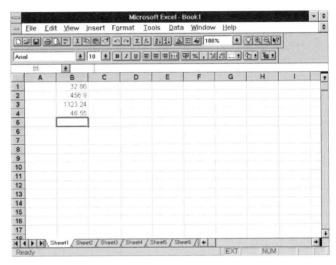

If you wanted to change the contents of a specific cell (say, B2), you'd do one of the following. Click in the cell and:

1. Press [F2], or

2. Click in the Formula Bar

When you do either of these, the [Enter] and [Cancel] boxes appear to the left of the Button Bar.

Excel 5.0 for Windows calls this state 'Edit Mode'. In Edit Mode the cursor keys produce different effects. Instead of moving you to alternate cells, they move through the contents of the active cell. Study the next illustration.

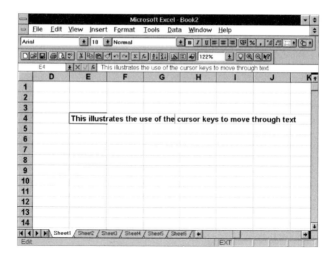

Here, some text has been entered into cell E4. Using the cursor keys now enables you to navigate through the text.

The text was split onto a second line by pressing [Alt]-RETURN.

In Edit Mode, you can also use the following keys:

Home
Moves the editing cursor to the start of an entry, or the beginning of the current line

End
Moves to the end of an entry, or to the end of the current line

Backspace
Deletes the character to the left of the cursor

Delete
Deletes the character to the right of the cursor

Cut and paste

You can perform cut and paste operations within cells. Click and hold with the left mouse button. Drag the editing cursor over the cell contents (usually text) which you want to copy or cut. Press [Ctrl]-[X] to cut it, or [Ctrl]-[C] to copy it. Move the insertion point to the new location and press [Ctrl]-[V] to paste the entry back in.

Entering large numbers

If you entered a number, say 4555892.7657, that was
too large for the current width of cell, then it would be
rounded up to 4555893. The Formula Bar would still
show the full number while the cell remained active.

If the number in a cell is particularly large, *Excel* will
often express it exponentially. 77777777777777, for
example, would be expressed, using scientific notation,
as 7.8E+13.

This is rather inconvenient. However, *Excel* hasn't
actually changed the number you've inserted: it's just
that, unless you tell it otherwise, it prefers to round
numbers up. You have two options here. You can alter
the way in which *Excel 5.0 for Windows* treats large
numbers, or you can increase the cell width.

Rounding numbers

With the cell active (but without having pressed [F2] to
enter Edit Mode), either pull down the [Format] menu
and choose [Cells], or press [Ctrl]-[I]. In the [Format
Cells] dialogue, click on the [Number] Tab.

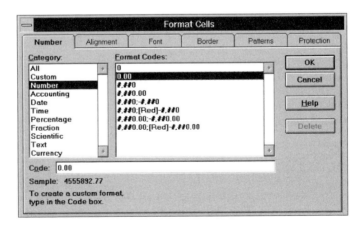

Select the correct entry in the [Category] list: in this case, [Number]. In the [Format Codes] box, highlight the number format you want to use. Click [OK].

 As you choose an entry in the [Format Codes] box, watch the [Sample] field to see what the original number looks like with the new formatting.

 If they won't fit inside a cell, *Excel* sometimes represents large numbers with ########, in spite of the format code you've applied (again, note that the original **Large** number itself is unaffected). This is *Excel's* way of rem- **numbers** inding you that you ought to amend the cell width (see 'Increasing Cell Width' on the next page).

With the Number Category selected, and a Format Code of 0.00, shortening the number to 45892.7657 would give us a result of 45892.77, fitting comfortably in the cell.

 There's a convenient short-cut menu route to the [Format Cells] dialogue. Right-click on the cell (or range of cells) you want to reformat. From the short-cut menu, **Format** select [Format Cells]. **cells**

Excel 5.0 for Windows also provides some useful buttons on its [Formatting] toolbar. The next illustration shows two.

Click here to increase decimals
(e.g. 896.00 becomes 896.000)

Click here to decrease decimals
(e.g. 991.00000 becomes 991.0000)

See 'Implementing Number Formatting Using Buttons' in Chapter 6 for information on further buttons. See 'Advanced Number Formatting' (also in

Chapter 6) for information on creating your own customised number formats.

Increasing column width

You can easily amend the width *Excel 5.0 for Windows* allocates to columns. You can't amend the width of individual cells, you can only amend all the cells with specified columns.

Changing the width of a single column

Do the following:

- Click inside one cell in the column you want to amend, or click on the column heading.
- Pull down the [Format] menu and select [Column], [Width].

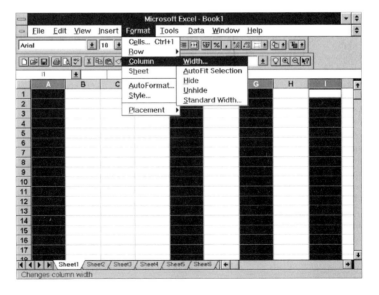

In the [Column Width] dialogue, enter a value in the [Column Width] field which represents the maximum number of characters (based on the current typeface) which a cell can hold.

Column width

There's a mouse short-cut, too. Move the pointer up to the top of the column you want to amend and position it in the column header, on the right column edge. The pointer changes to a cross.

Click and hold with the left mouse button. Drag the column to the right to increase its width (or to the left to decrease it). To conceal the column, drag the right edge inwards past the left.

Release the button to confirm the operation.

Changing multiple columns

Click anywhere in the heading of the first column. Hold down the mouse button and drag the selection to include neighbouring columns.

You can select non-adjacent columns. To do this, hold down [Ctrl] and click in the relevant column headings.

Pull down the [Format] menu and select [Column], [Width]. Amend the [Column Width] dialogue as per the 'Changing the Width of a Single Column' section above.

Using *Excel's* 'Best Fit' feature

You can also automate column width. This is a useful feature when you've already defined one or more non-standard cells.

As we have seen, if an over large number is entered, *Excel 5.0 for Windows* replaces it with #######, to indicate that the column needs widening.

You can still see the full number in the Formula Bar.

To make the whole of the column adjust to fit, do the following. Pull down the [Format] menu and select [Column], [AutoFit Selection].

Best fit

There's a mouse short-cut for this, too. Position the mouse cursor on the right edge of the column heading; the cursor becomes a cross. Double-click with the left mouse button. The column expands to accommodate the full number.

Amending the default column width

You can also stipulate the width (in characters) which all columns within a sheet – except for any you've amended manually – should have. Pull down the [Format] menu, choose [Column], [Standard Width].

In the [Standard Width] dialogue, enter a value in the [Standard Column Width] field which represents the maximum number of characters (based on the current typeface) which a cell can hold. Click on [OK] when you've finished.

Creating a sample worksheet

Now it's time to put what we've learned so far into action. On the way, we'll explore entering text into worksheet cells, and amending row height.

Let's say we want to create a worksheet which will provide a simple bank statement. With *Excel 5.0 for Windows*, this is a straightforward process. What fields do we need to include?

It's always advisable to plan out a worksheet before you create it; this can save you a lot of work.

We need (as an absolute minimum) the following:

- A column representing deposits
- A column representing withdrawals
- A column carrying a description of each transaction
- A column carrying the transaction date
- A row totalling deposits
- A row totalling withdrawals
- A row providing the balance (deposits minus withdrawals)

This sounds complicated, but isn't.

There are other things we need, too. These are all factors which may not be strictly necessary but which will improve the appearance of our worksheet.

- An overall worksheet heading
- Column headings
- Special formatting for selected rows

In this section, and in subsequent chapters, we'll create the basics of this worksheet. We'll also refine it along the way.

Inserting the heading

Inserting the heading

Press [Ctrl]-[N] to create a new workbook. As the first step, we'll create the sheet heading. Move the mouse pointer over the row heading Row 2 and click on the heading to select the entire row. Alternatively, click within any cell in Row 2.

Pull down the [Format] menu and select [Row], [Height]. In the [Height] dialogue, enter [35] in the [Row Height] field. Choose [OK] when you've finished. Row 2 is now taller.

You can use a 'best fit' approach to row height. To do this, select the row. Pull down the [Format] menu and choose [Row], [AutoFit].

Row 2 has been made taller by entering a higher value for its height in the [Row Height] field.

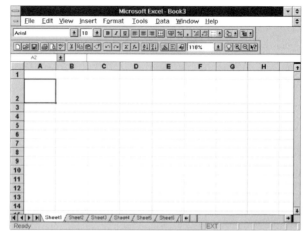

For more general information on using AutoFit, see 'Using *Excel*'s Best Fit Feature' earlier.

We shall need to widen some of the cells in Row 2 to accommodate the heading. Move the mouse pointer over the column heading for Column C. Left-click and hold. Drag the selection to encompass Columns C and D. Release the mouse button. Move the pointer over the right heading edge of Column D; it changes into a cross. Drag the columns outwards, as far as the left edge of column E. Release the button to confirm.

Click inside cell C2 and press [F2] to enter Edit Mode. Type in [Transaction]. Press ENTER to confirm. Click in D2. Press [F2] and type in [Inventory]. Press ENTER again. The text will appear in the cells, but we need to apply the relevant typeface and type size. Click within C2 again and hold down the mouse button; drag the selection to include D2.

**Selected
cells**

Selection 'reverses' cells, i.e. they're shown as white on black, rather than *vice versa* (see Chapter 5 for more information on selection). Note, however, that although both B2 and C2 are now selected, B2 isn't reversed. This is always true of the first cell of any selection. You can tell the first cell is selected, though, by the fact that it has a selection border round it.

Pull down the [Format] menu and select [Cells]. The [Format Cells] dialogue launches.

*Click on the [Font]
tab. Select the
appropriate font in
the [Font] list, and
the type size in the
[Size] list. I
suggest Arial 24pt.
Click on [OK] when
you've finished.*

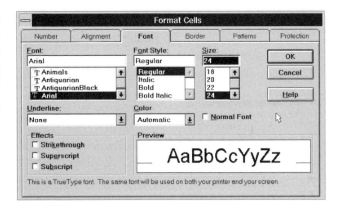

This is the result.

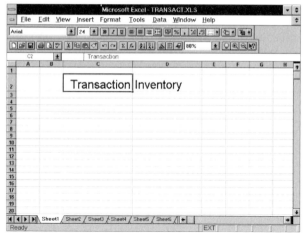

We can improve on this in two ways.

1. Click within C2. Click on the [Align Right] button in the overhead Formatting toolbar. The [Transaction] is now flush with the right column edge.

2. We can remove the cell borders in row 2. This will make the heading visually more effective. To do this, click in cell A2. Hold down one SHIFT key as you press [Ctrl] together with the right cursor key; this automatically selects the whole of row 2. Pull down the [Format Cells] dialogue again but this time click on the [Border] tab.

Click once in the [Left] box in the [Border] section; a line appears. Click on the down-pointing arrow to the right of the [Color] field. In the list of colours which appears, click on the white square. Choose [OK] to confirm. The left and right edges of all the cells within row 2 disappear.

Inserting column sub-headings

As we've already seen, you can easily insert text into *Excel 5.0 for Windows* cells. However, *Excel* also lets you apply a variety of colours and/or patterns to selected cells, and we'll use this feature to enliven the sub-headings.

Use fills to divide headings from worksheet contents, for enhanced impact.

We need four columns in our worksheet, for the following categories:

- Transaction date
- Details (optional)
- Deposit
- Withdrawal

Click in cell B5. Press [F2] and type in [Date]. Press ENTER. Repeat this process for cells C5:E5 (i.e. C5, D5 and E5), typing in respectively [Details], [Deposit] and [Withdrawal].

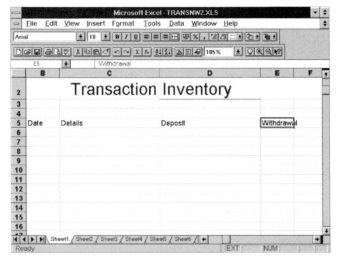

Clearly, we need to make some changes to the worksheet design. Column D is too wide, and E too narrow. And the text needs to be realigned within the cells. We'll rectify these shortly. First, click and hold on cell B5. Drag the selection as far as E5. Pull down the [Format] menu and select [Cells]. In the [Format Cells] dialogue, click on the [Patterns] tab.

Click on the down-pointing arrow to the right of the [Pattern] box; click on the pattern you want to apply to the selected cells.

If you want to apply a colour, choose it either from the [Color] palette, or from the [Pattern] drop-down list. You can also combine colours with patterns.

When you've finished, choose [OK]. Now do the following

1.   Click on the right edge of the column heading for column D. Drag the edge inwards so that it stops just to the right of [Inventory].

2.   Click on the right edge of the column heading for column E. Drag the edge outwards, as far as the left edge of column F.

3.   Select cells B5:E5 (B5, C5, D5 and E5); see earlier for how to do this. Click on the [Center] button in the Formatting toolbar. Click on the [Bold] button.

This is the result so far.

Remember to save your work so far. Press [Ctrl]-[S].

If you haven't yet saved your work, *Excel 5.0 for Windows* prompts you to allocate a name. Complete the [Save As] dialogue as necessary, and click on [OK] to confirm the operation.

In the next chapter, we'll start to insert values and formulae.

Editing and refining worksheets

You can edit and refine worksheets – learn how here! You'll insert formulae and use AutoFill to create basic cell series. Now format your worksheet and insert/delete components. Use Format Painter to automate formatting. Finally, master the selection of worksheet components.

5

Editing and refining worksheets

In this chapter, we'll develop the simple worksheet we started to create in Chapter 4.

Developing the worksheet

To load up the sample worksheet we were working on in Chapter 4:

1.   Pull down the [File] menu and choose [Open].

2.   In the [Open] dialogue, select the relevant directory in the [Directories] box.

3.   Enter the file name. Choose [OK].

So far, we've concentrated on the overall worksheet layout. However, there are still some formatting changes we can profitably make to the sheet. For instance, we can add some text clarifying cell C43. We'll handle these as we come to them. First, let's look at formulae. We need to insert some which will automatically return the values of specific cells.

Formula

A formula is a cell entry which describes how other values relate to each other. Another way of looking at it is to say that formulae carry out mathematical operations on values entered into cells.

Formulae can contain constants and cell coordinates (or names, see Chapter 7). We need to insert three formulae:

- One to return the total number of deposits

- One to return the total number of withdrawals

- One to return the difference between the total number of deposits and the total number of withdrawals

When you insert a formula into a cell, it isn't normally visible. What you see is the result of the mathematical operation itself. When you select the cell, however, the formula displays in the Formula Bar.

Deriving a total

Scroll down your worksheet until you reach a row which is at some distance from the headings. For instance, if you want your worksheet to log a month's worth of transactions (which seems reasonable), move to row 40. All formulae begin with [=], so click in cell D40 and press [=].

Excel automatically opens Edit Mode (see page 51). An [=] appears in the Formula Bar, and the [Enter] and [Cancel] boxes appear to the left of the Button Bar. Type in: SUM(D6:D39). This formula totals the cells from D6 to D39. The components of this formula are:

- Sum

- Brackets

- Equals

Sum

Summation is one of the most frequently used *Excel* functions (see Chapter 9). SUM returns the total of all the values in a given range. Most frequently, you'll use SUM to total columns and rows.

Brackets, ( )

Functions are always followed by brackets. In this case, [SUM] requires that its cell references etc. should be enclosed in parentheses.

Equals, =

[=] is probably the most common mathematical operator. Other common examples are:

[+] Addition

[-] Subtraction

[*] Multiplication

[/] Division

[^] Exponentials

Examples of simple operators

There is a 'pecking order' to the way in which *Excel* performs mathematical operations. Look at the following instance:

=2*12+36

The total of this is 60, not 96. In other words, *Excel* performs the multiplication first (2*12) and then adds 36 to the result. The way to make *Excel* produce the correct answer is to enclose a section of the numbers in parentheses:

=2*(12+36)

This tells *Excel* to add 12 and 36 and to multiply the result by 2. This distinction can be even more acute with exponentials:

=2^4

This is 16 (i.e. 2 to the power of 4). Compare this with the next example:

=2^4+18

Here, without brackets *Excel* produces 34. With brackets, however, the result can be very different.

=2^(4+18)

produces 4,194,304

The simple rule is that *Excel* performs multiplication and division before addition and subtraction, unless parentheses are used. When you've entered the formula, press RETURN or click on the [Enter] box.

The [Enter] box is the button containing a green tick which appears next to the Formula Bar.

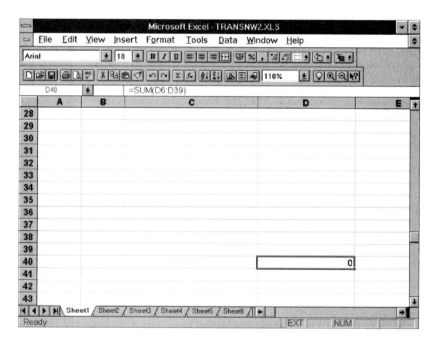

Notice that D40 displays [0], because no values have yet been entered in D6:D39, while the Formula Bar shows the formula.

Inserting a formula for a total

To insert the formula for the total number of withdrawals, click within E40. Press [=], to activate Formula Edit Mode. Type in:

SUM(E6:E39)

Press RETURN or click on the [Enter] box. This is exactly the same procedure which we used in 'Inserting the Formula for the Total Number of Deposits', earlier. However, there is an alternative route: AutoFill.

Using AutoFill

This is probably the easiest method to use here. AutoFill is a tool for creating series (see Chapter 9), copying data or – in this case – cloning formulae. Here's how to use it.

The menu route

Click and hold in D40. Drag the selection to the right to include E40. Pull down the [Edit] menu and select [Fill], [Series]. Select [AutoFill] in the [Type] section of the [Series] dialogue. Click on [OK] when you've finished.

You can also achieve the same result here by pulling down the [Edit] menu and selecting [Fill], [Right]. Alternatively, press [Ctrl]-[R]. [Ctrl]-[L] would fill selected cells to the left.

Excel's [Fill] command fills rows or columns of cells with the contents of a single cell which can be located either at the beginning or end of the row/column.

Fill

You can also use [Fill] before you've entered anything into the row or column. Select the relevant cells and then type in a value. Press RETURN and then pull down the [Edit] menu. Select [Up], [Down], [Right] or [Left] as appropriate.

Both [Fill] and [AutoFill] are valid here.

The mouse route

If you look at D40, you'll see a small black box on the bottom right hand corner. This is the Fill Handle. Any cell – or range of cells – which you select has this. Here's how to use the Fill Handle. With D40 selected, move the mouse pointer over the handle; it changes into a cross. Drag the handle to encompass E40. When you release the mouse button, *Excel* copies the formula within D40 to E40.

Excel also updates the cell references, changing the formula from `=SUM(D6:D39)` to `=SUM(E6:E39)`. This is the advantage of using AutoFill.

If you hold down the [Ctrl] key as you drag the Fill Handle, *Excel* inserts an identical sequence of entries rather than a series. For instance, dragging D40's handle to E40 while holding down [Ctrl] would insert the same formula, `=SUM(D6:D39)`, into E40; *Excel* doesn't update the cell references. See 'Using the Fill handle' in Chapter 9 for more information.

Inserting a formula for a difference

To insert the formula for the difference between the total number of deposits and the total number of withdrawals, scroll down to cell D43. Click in it to select it. Press [=] and type in **D40-E40**. Press RETURN or click on the Enter box next to the Formula Bar.

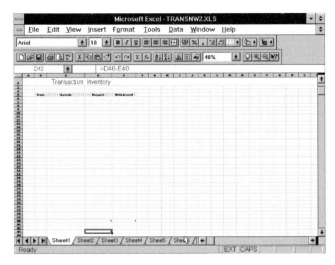

Completing the worksheet formatting

We can do the following to make the sheet clearer:

1. Insert some text clarifying D43

2. Amend the colour of selected cell borders, for emphasis

3. Amend the colour of cell text (for instance, we can colour the values returned in the totals differently from the data values, to enhance the impact.

2. and 3. are dealt with in Chapter 6. We'll deal with 1. shortly. First, let's look at how to delete worksheet components, and insert rows or columns.

Deleting worksheet elements

Deletion is a straightforward process in *Excel*. There are two basic approaches to bear in mind. You can delete the contents of cells within rows and columns (*Excel* calls this 'clearing'), or you can delete the underlying cell structure, too.

Deleting cell contents

To delete the contents of a selected cell, or range of cells, while leaving the cell structure intact, press [Delete].

If column A has a number of values, and you've selected it by clicking on the column heading, pressing [Delete] clears all the cells. There is also a menu route. With the cell (or column/row) selected, pull down the [Edit] menu and select [Clear].

The resulting sub-menu provides four options:

- All
- Formats
- Contents
- Notes

We'll explore these here.

All

Selecting [All] deletes the following:

- Values
- Cell formatting
- Notes (explored in Chapter 7).

but doesn't delete the cell structure.

Formats

In the next illustration, A7 has had a coloured border and fill applied. (Advanced cell formatting is discussed in Chapter 6; fills are explored in Chapter 4). A value has also been inserted.

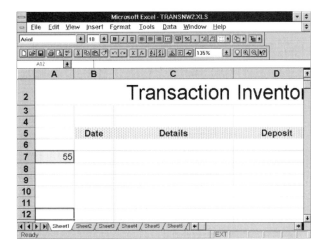

Selecting the cell and choosing [Edit], [Clear], [Formats] will remove the colour and fill, but leave the value intact.

Contents

This is the equivalent of pressing [Delete].

Deleting cell structures and contents

The procedures are slightly different here, depending on whether you're deleting individual cells or cell ranges, or columns/rows.

Deleting cells and cell ranges

Select the cell or cell range (see 'Selection Procedures' later for information on advanced selection). Pull down the [Edit] menu and choose [Delete].

In the [Delete] dialogue, select either [Shift Cells Left] or [Shift Cells Up].

Shift cells

This prompts the cells which haven't been erased to take the place of those which have by moving to the left. This makes surviving cells achieve the same effect by moving up. Choose [OK] when you've finished.

Deleting columns or rows

Either:

1. Select one cell within the column or row you need to delete.

2. Pull down the [Delete] dialogue (see above).

3. Choose [Entire Row] or [Entire Column], as appropriate

4. Click on [OK] to confirm

or:

1. Click on the column or row header; this select the entire column or row.

2. Pull down the [Edit] menu and choose [Delete].

The second method above doesn't launch the [Delete] dialogue: *Excel* simply deletes the row or column immediately.

Inserting columns/rows

Click in the heading of the row or column where you want to carry out the insertion.

You can select multiple rows or columns by dragging the mouse over their headings.

Pull down the [Insert] menu and choose [Rows] or [Columns]. Alternatively, press [Ctrl]- SHIFT-[+], or right-click on the selected row and column and choose [Insert] from the short-cut menu which launches.

Inserting text clarifying C43

Back to our sample worksheet. This is the final formatting step here; Chapter 6 will pick up where this Chapter leaves off. Click in C43. Press [F2] to enter Edit Mode. Type in the following:

```
Residue
```

Press RETURN to confirm, or click on the Enter box
next to the Formula Bar; *Excel* moves the cursor to
C44. Click within C43 again. Press [F2]. Click on the
[Bold] button in the overhead [Formatting] toolbar.
Click on the [Centre] button.

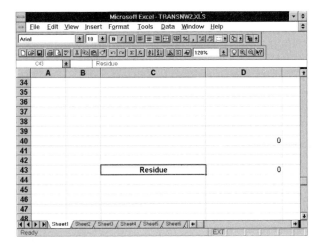

We now need to colour C43 so that it matches the other
headings: B5:E5. We could follow the procedure set out
in 'Inserting Column Sub-Headings' in Chapter 4.
However, here's another technique.

Using Format Painter

Format Painter is a useful tool for copying formats
from selected cells and applying them to others. It
automates the entire process. Here's how to use
Format Painter. Select any cell in B5:E5. Click on the
[Format Painter] button in the [Standard] toolbar.

Format Painter
button

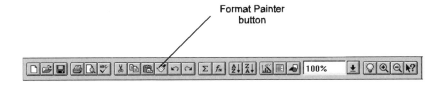

The cell you've selected is surrounded with a moving border, and the cursor becomes a cross complete with a paintbrush icon. Click in C43; *Excel* 'pastes in' the original formatting. The Format Painter button doesn't copy the formatting to the *Windows* Clipboard.

Clipboard

The Clipboard is a section of your computer's internal memory set aside for the temporary storage of copies of text and graphics. Items stored in the Clipboard remain there until you copy another item or close *Windows*.

If you double-click on the [Format Painter] button instead of single-clicking on it, you can transfer the same format to more than one destination. Simply click in as many destination cells or cell ranges as you need. To terminate Format Painter, click on the button again.

Note that Format Painter copies ALL formatting information. This means that, in this instance, it also copies information on:

* Font
* Type size
* Alignment

In other words, we needn't have applied these manually (see above). Format Painter does it all.

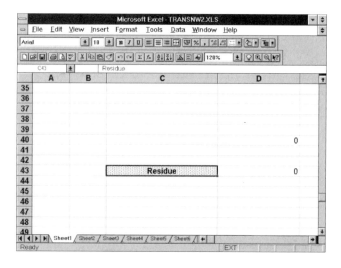

All You Need To Know About
Excel 5.0 for Windows

We'll return to this worksheet in Chapter 6.

Save your worksheet

Make sure you save your worksheet! Press [Ctrl]-[S]. If you haven't yet saved your work during this session, *Excel* prompts you to allocate a name. Complete the [Save As] dialogue as necessary, and click on [OK] to confirm it.

Selection procedures

In earlier chapters (in particular, Chapter 3), we've looked at the question of selection in passing. Now we need to look at it in more detail. First, however, since selection is often concerned with groups of cells, we'll discuss 'ranges'.

Ranges

Ranges are rectangular sections of worksheets. They are described in *Excel* by referring to:

1. The upper left cell reference
2. The lower right cell reference

Both are separated by a colon. In the illustration below, the group of cells whose upper left cell is C3, and whose lower right reference is E6, is a simple range. This is described as C3:E6.

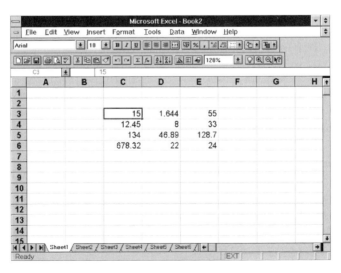

In earlier chapters, we've used this method principally to describe sections of rows or columns. However, it's probably more usual to use it to identify ranges.

Excel operates by selection. The principle is: target and then shoot. *Excel* needs you to identify 'objects' (in the broadest sense) before you can modify or manipulate them. Selection is therefore crucial to the way *Excel* works. In this section, we'll first recap on the basic selection techniques we've discussed on-the-fly in earlier chapters. Then we'll discuss some more advanced techniques.

Basic selection

Excel lets you select data in a variety of ways.

Selecting single cells

Click in a cell to select it. Or use the cursor keys to move the cell pointer over it.

Selecting ranges

Click in the first cell in the range. Hold down the left mouse button and drag over the cells you want to include.

There's a keyboard route, too. Use the cursor keys to move the cell pointer over the first cell. Hold down one SHIFT key as you use the appropriate cursor keys to extend the selection. You can also do this in a slightly different way. Move the cell pointer over the first cell. Press [F8] to enter *Excel's* Extend mode. *Excel* inserts [EXT] in the Status bar.

Now use the cursor keys to extend the selection. To get out of Extend mode, press [F8] again, or [Esc].

Selecting non-adjacent ranges

Here, two ranges are shown: C3:E6 A11:B13

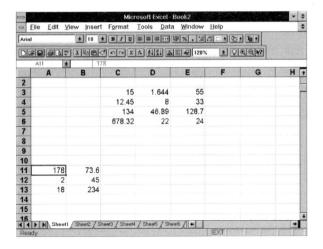

If we wanted to perform the identical operation on both ranges (for instance, applying the same cell border and/or fill), we could do so in a variety of ways. For instance, we could select each range individually, and go through the same steps each time. This is undoubtedly the least convenient method. Or we could format one range and then use Format Painter (see 'Using Format Painter' earlier).

However, there is an easier and more straightforward method: we can select both ranges simultaneously. Here's how to do this. Select the first range, using any of the techniques we've just discussed (with the exception of Extend mode). Then hold down [Ctrl] as you select the second.

Non-adjacent ranges

Excel employs a special notation to describe non-adjacent ranges: it separates them with commas. The ranges in the preceding illustration would be: `C3:E6,A11:B13` The component ranges are separated by commas.

Selecting a row

Click on the row heading. To de-select it, simply click in another cell which is outside the row.

There's a keyboard route. Use the cursor keys to select one of the cells in the relevant row. Press SHIFT-SPACEBAR. To de-select the row, cursor out of it.

Selecting a column

Click on the column heading. To de-select it, simply click in another cell which is outside the column.

There's a keyboard route. Use the cursor keys to select one of the cells in the relevant column. Press [Ctrl]-SPACEBAR. To de-select the column, cursor out of it.

Useful short-cuts

Excel offers several short-cuts which make selection easier, and more specific:

Extending selection

Press [Ctrl]-SHIFT-[*] to select a cell range when one of the constituent cells has been selected.

Selecting large ranges

If a range is especially large, here's an alternative selection technique you can use. Click in the cell in one corner. Scroll to the opposite corner. Hold down one SHIFT key then click in the corner cell here.

Selecting ranges on more than one worksheet

If you need to apply specific formatting to the same area on more than one worksheet, *Excel* makes this easy. Hold down [Ctrl] as you click on the relevant worksheet tabs. Then select the cells you want to format. Whatever formatting you apply now will be duplicated in all the selected sheets.

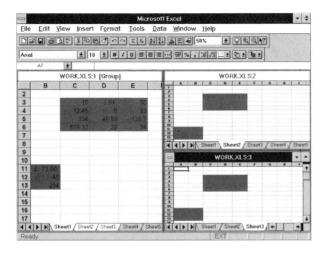

This is a tiled view of three sheets after the cell ranges have been coloured red (for more information on tiling windows, see 'Cascading and Tiling Windows' in Chapter 2).

Selecting multiple rows or columns

Click on the row or column heading. Now do either of these:

1. Hold down the left mouse button and drag to select adjacent rows or columns. Release the mouse button to confirm.

2. Hold down one SHIFT key and use the cursor keys to select adjacent rows or columns.

Selecting the whole of a worksheet

Press [Ctrl]-[A]. Or click on the [Select All] button at the intersection of the row and column headings. See 'Select All Button' in Chapter 3 for more information.

Selecting Worksheets

Selecting worksheets is easy. Simply click on a sheet tab at the base of the *Excel* screen to make the associated sheet active. The name on the active sheet tab is always bold. If you need to select more than one sheet at a time, do the following:

1. If the sheets are adjacent, click on the first. Then hold down a SHIFT key as you click on the last; *Excel* selects the intervening sheets, as well.

2.   If the sheets aren't adjacent, click on the first. Then hold down [Ctrl] as you click on the sheets.

Grouping worksheets

Excel calls multiple selection of worksheets 'grouping'. The advantage to grouping is that it enables you to carry out formatting operations on all of the selected sheets at once. This saves time and effort. This is especially useful for worksheets which share a common look (e.g. the same column and/or row headings). You can organise sheets into a group whenever you need to; when you've finished formatting them, you can easily return them to normal.

Ungrouping worksheets

There are three ways to ungroup sheets:

1.   Click on a tab that is not part of the group.

2.   Click on the active sheet tab as you hold down one SHIFT key.

3.   Right-click on one of the sheet tabs. *Excel* produces a short-cut menu (Short-cut menus provide rapid and convenient access to common *Excel* menu commands. For more information on short-cut menus, see Chapter 3). Choose [Ungroup Sheets].

Right-click with the mouse over any sheet tab. In the short-cut menu which appears, choose [Select All Sheets].

Selecting other *Excel* objects

Excel lets you insert a variety of additional objects into worksheets. These can include graphics images and charts (see Chapter 11 for more information on these) or linked files from another application (for more information on object linking, see Chapter 11). As with everything in *Excel*, you need to select objects before you can manipulate or reformat them.

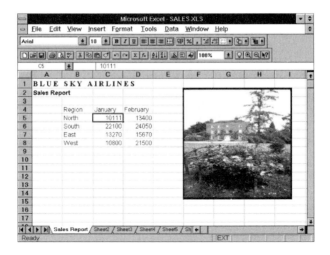

To work with an inserted graphic image, you need to select it first. Click anywhere within the image; *Excel* surrounds it with black selection handles. See Chapter 11 for how to work with graphics images etc.

Selecting specific cell types

1.   To make *Excel* search through the whole of a worksheet in order to select the cells you specify, select one cell first. To search through a specific range, select this in the normal way.

2.   Pull down the [Edit] menu and select [Go To]. (see 'Using Go To' in Chapter 4 for information on how to use [Go To] to jump to specific cell coordinates). Or press [F5].

3.   Click on [Special].

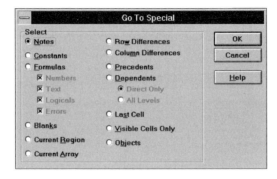

4.   In the [Go To Special] dialogue, choose the type of cell you want to select. For instance, if you want to select all cells which contain formulae, choose [Formulas]. Then check the appropriate formula sub-categories. If you want to search for formulae which produce numbers, choose [Numbers]. If you want to find all formulae which are incorrect (i.e. they produce error values), check [Errors].

The resulting selection can contain many cells and ranges. Here are some brief notes on the other available options.

Precedents and dependents

[Precedents] selects cells which are referenced by the active cell. These are cells which are part of formulae. For instance, if a cell has the following formula:

=SUM(C6+C7)

then C6 and C7 are precedents.

[Dependents] selects cells whose formula refer to the active cell. Dependents are cells whose formulae refer to other cells. For instance, if the active cell is A5, [Dependents] would select all cells which refer to A5.

Excel always searches the entire worksheet.

Notes

Choose this to select all cells which contain a note. For more information on cell notes, see Chapter 7.

 There's a useful keyboard short-cut here. Press [Ctrl]-SHIFT-[?] directly from within your worksheet.

Constants

This selects all cells whose values do not start with [=].

Blanks

This selects all empty cells.

Current Region

By 'region', *Excel* means a rectangular area, bounded by empty rows and columns, around the active cell.

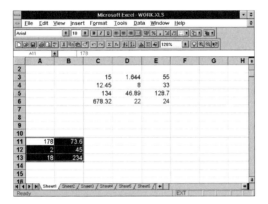

If cell B11 is active when you choose [Current Region], *Excel* selects the range of which it forms part (because it's surrounded by empty rows and columns). There's a handy keyboard short-cut. Press [Ctrl-[*] directly from within your work-sheet. Note that this is the asterisk on the numerical key pad, not the asterisk over the number 8.

Current Array

This selects the whole array, if any, to which the active cell belongs. For more information on arrays, see Chapter 9. Press [Ctrl]-[/] directly from within your worksheet to search for any current array.

Row Differences

Choose this to select cells within the same row whose reference pattern is different. Press [Ctrl]-[\] directly from within your worksheet.

Column Differences

Choose this to select cells within the same column whose reference pattern is different. Press [Ctrl]-SHIFT-[|]

Last Cell

Choose this to select the final cell in the current
worksheet which contains data and/or formatting.

Visible Cells

Use this to select visible cells only. Some cells in *Excel*
worksheets can be hidden. For more information on
hidden cells, see Chapter 7.

Objects

Choose this to select all graphic objects (e.g. clip art and
charts).

6

Advanced worksheets

Now you're ready for advanced formatting! You can fine tune the way *Excel* handles numbers, customise worksheet formatting, turn grid lines on and off and carry out spelling checks to get your spreadsheet looking the way you want it! Then create workspaces for ease of use.

All You Need To Know About
Excel 5.0 for Windows

Advanced worksheets

In this chapter we'll continue formatting our Transaction Register worksheet.

Advanced formatting

We've already examined various formatting features on-the-fly, during the course of this book so far. Now let's look at formatting in more detail.

Advanced number formatting

We looked at basic number formatting in Chapter 4 (see the 'Rounding Numbers' section). This section supplements this with some advanced techniques.

Number formatting using buttons

There are several buttons on the [Formatting] toolbar which provide useful routes:

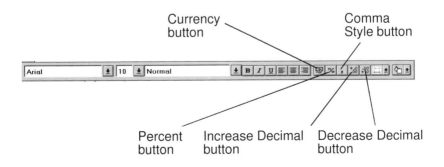

Currency button

Select the relevant cell or cell ranges. Click on the [Currency] button. This applies the currently defined Currency style.

Styles

Styles are collections of associated formatting commands which you can apply *en masse* to individual cells or cell ranges. For example, if you want numbers of cells within your current worksheet to share the same formatting, you can apply a style which contains all of the formatting commands to them.

The advantages of using styles (as opposed to Format Painter, for instance) are speed and convenience. If you want to change any aspect of the associated formatting, you amend the style; *Excel 5.0 for Windows* then looks through your worksheet and amends every instance of the style automatically, and quickly. See Chapter 10 for more information on *Excel*'s use of styles.

Percent button

Select the relevant cell or cell ranges. Click on the [Percent] button so that *Excel* applies the currently defined Percent style.

Comma style button

Select the relevant cell or cell ranges. Click on the [Comma Style] button for the currently defined Comma style. This applies commas and two decimal places to numbers.

Increase decimal and decrease decimal buttons

These have been covered in the 'Rounding Numbers' section in Chapter 4.

Creating custom number formats

Excel lets you create your own number formats. Pull down the [Format] menu and select [Cells].

You can also right-click anywhere in the worksheet to produce the associated short-cut menu. Choose [Format Cells].

In the [Format Cells] dialogue, click on the [Number] tab. Now use the [Category] and [Format Codes] sections to pick the existing number format which is closest to what you need. When you've done this, click in the [Code] field.

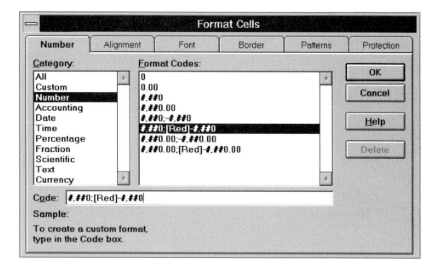

Amend the codes as required. Below are brief details of some of the principal codes.

A digit placeholder

If there are more digits to the right of the decimal point than [#]s in corresponding position in the format, *Excel* rounds the number down accordingly. If there are too many digits to the left, *Excel* displays them anyway.

0 (zero) A digit placeholder.

This is almost the same as [#]. Here's the difference. If there are more zeros in the format than are present in the number, *Excel* displays them. This makes numbers like 139.8 display as 139.80

? A digit placeholder.

This is almost identical to the zero. The difference is alignment. If [?]s appear in a format, *Excel* makes decimal points align (by including extra spaces).

Full stop

The precise placement of the [.] tells *Excel* how many digits should appear on either side of the decimal point.

%

Excel converts the number to a percentage, inserts [%].

Comma

If [,] appears in a format surrounded by [#]s or zeros, *Excel 5.0 for Windows* inserts commas to separate thousands.

E- E+ e- e+

If any of these are present in a format, the number is displayed using scientific notation. [E] or [e] is inserted.

@

This is a text placeholder. If [@] appears in a format and text has been inserted into the cell, *Excel* displays it in the format in place of the [@].

Colours

If colours are specified in a format, *Excel 5.0 for Windows* displays the relevant characters in the specified colour.

If you need further assistance with number format syntax, consult *Excel's* on line help.

Advanced cell formatting

Look at the next illustration.

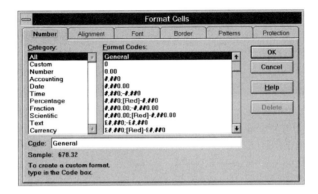

This is the [Format Cells] dialogue. We've encountered
it several times before (see Chapter 4 et al). It's
currently displaying its [Number] tab. In this section
we'll look at the other tabs (some of these have already
been explored in passing).

To reach the [Format Cells] dialogue, first select the
cells you want to format. Then do either of the
following:

1.   Pull down the [Format] menu and select [Cells].

2.   Right-click anywhere within the selected cells.
Choose [Format Cells] from the shortcut menu which
appears.

Alignment tab

[Alignment] determines the way in which text and
numbers display within cells.

By default, text within cells displays from the left,
numbers from the right.

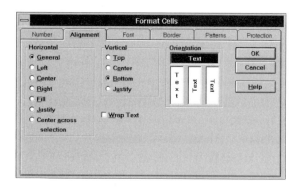

It does so under two main headings: [Horizontal] and [Vertical]. The [Horizontal] alignment commands are:

General The default. Text is aligned left, numbers to the right

Left Cell contents are displayed from the left.

Centre Cell contents are centred within the cell

Right Cell contents are displayed from the right

Fill Cell contents are duplicated until the cell is full

Justify Combines [Left] and [Right]

Centre across selection Cell contents are centred across however many cells are selected

The effects of applying [Justify] are only visible if you have more than one line of 'wrapped' text. See 'Applying Text Wrap' on the next page.

The [Vertical] commands are:

Top Cell contents follow the top of the cell

Centre Cell contents are clustered in the middle of the cell

Bottom Cell contents follow the bottom of the cell

Justify Cell contents are justified along the top and bottom of the cell

Most of these are also found in word processors. However, there's another aspect to [Alignment] which is more or less unique to spreadsheets. You can specify 'orientation'. This refers to the direction of text flow.

Using [Alignment]

Select the cell or cell range you want to align. Pull down the [Format Cells] dialogue. Select the [Horizontal], [Vertical] and [Orientation] options you require. Choose [OK] when you've finished.

You can 'mix and match' here: *Excel* accepts permutations.

Applying text wrap

Excel 5.0 for Windows lets you 'wrap' multiple lines of text within a cell.

Normally, if there is too much text within a cell, *Excel* simply extends it beyond the cell border, in one long line. Look at the next pair of illustrations.

Text that is not wrapped   *Wrapped text*
                                   [Horizontal] and [Vertical] settings are
                                   [General] and [Bottom], respectively

On the left, *Excel* is displaying a long text string which starts in D8 and continues to G8. If you want to display this as multiple lines within the one cell ('word wrap'), do the following:

1. Select the cell range which contains the text (in this case, D8:G8).

2. In the [Alignment] tab of the [Format Cells] dialogue, choose [Wrap Text], followed by [OK].

If you amend the width of a cell which contains wrapped text, the text realigns accordingly.

Font tab

We've already discussed the use of the [Font] tab to impose typeface and type sizes on cell text (see 'Inserting the Heading' in Chapter 4). You can also use it to set text colour. We'll apply this to our sample worksheet.

Load up the worksheet we worked on in Chapter 5. (If you're unsure of how to do this, see 'Developing our Worksheet' in Chapter 5.) Let's insert some values into the body of the sheet; this will enable us to see what further formatting changes are needed.

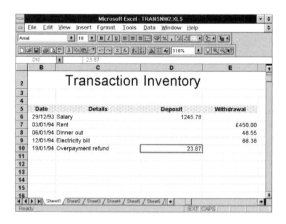

It would be useful to have the cells containing the new totals distinguished from the others. *Excel 5.0 for Windows* makes this easy: you can apply colours to cells. Here's how to do this.

Select the cell or cell ranges you want to colour (in this case, D40, D43 and E40).

 You can select multiple cells by holding down one [Ctrl] key as you click in them.

Activate the [Font] tab in the [Format Cells] dialogue. Click on the down-pointing arrow to the right of the [Color] field; *Excel 5.0 for Windows* produces a drop-down list of available colours.

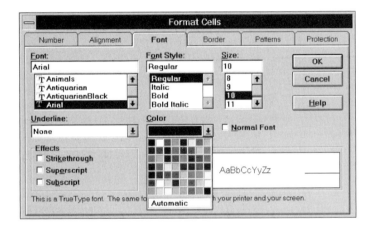

Click on the colour you want in order to apply it. In our case, we'll choose blue. Click on [OK] when you've finished.

We can carry out a similar process in respect of the [Deposit] and [Withdrawal] columns: if we make the cells in each a different colour, this will aid differentiation. Select D6:D39. Invoke the [Font] tab and follow the procedures outlined above to apply a colour to the [Deposit] cells. Choose red. Click on [OK] when you've finished.

Select E6:E39. Repeat the above procedure and choose green. Click on [OK]. Save the latest amendments to your worksheet.

Border tab

We've encountered the [Border] tab in Chapter 4
('Inserting the Heading' section), where we removed
the cell borders in row 2. Now we'll take this several
steps further. We'll:

1. Add emphasis to the Total cells

2. Surround the worksheet with an outline

Emphasising the totals

Select D40, D43 and E40. Invoke the [Border] tab from
the [Format Cells] dialogue. In the [Styles] section,
choose the appropriate border style (in this case, the
style on the bottom left). Now click once in the [Left],
[Right], [Top] and [Bottom] fields.

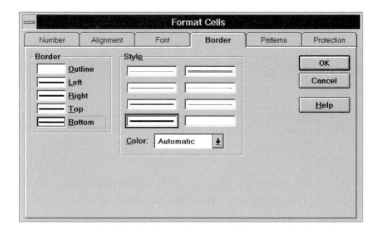

Choose [OK] when you're finished. You can see the
result on the next page.

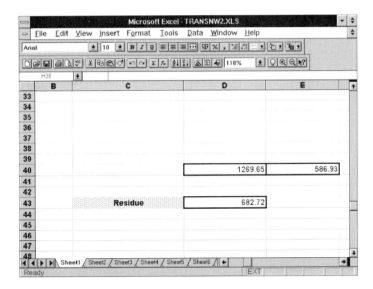

Outlining the worksheet

Select B2:E43. Invoke the [Border] tab. In the [Styles] section, choose the double-line style. In the [Border] section, click once in [Outline].

 If the [Left], [Right], [Top] and [Bottom] fields are filled with grey, click in them twice to clear them.

Choose [OK].

Borders

If you find that applying the outline to your worksheet has restored the borders in cells B2:E2 (we hid them in 'Inserting the Heading' in Chapter 4), do the following. Click in one cell. Invoke the [Border] tab. Click on the down-pointing arrow to the right of the [Color] field. In the graphic drop down list which appears, select the white square. Click in the [Left] or [Right] fields in the [Border] section, as appropriate. For instance, if you're working with B2, choose [Right] to hide the right cell border. Choose [OK] to confirm.

Repeat this as necessary.

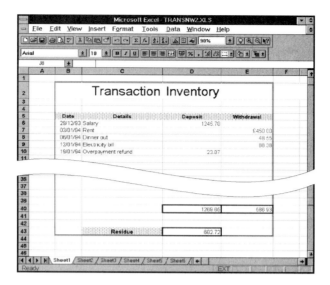

This completes the basis of our sample worksheet.
We'll come back to it from time to time in future
chapters.

Gridlines

By default, *Excel 5.0 for Windows* displays horizontal
and vertical lines within worksheets to mark cell and
column/row boundaries. However, you can hide them
if you want. You can also specify whether they print or
not (irrespective of whether they're visible); see
Chapter 8 for more information on printing.

Hiding gridlines

Pull down the [Tools] menu and select [Options]. In the
[Options] dialogue, click on the [View] tab. The
[Options] dialogue is used to configure a wide variety of
Excel features; see Chapter 12 for more information.

 Turning off gridlines through the [Options] dialogue also
stops them from printing.

Deselect the [Gridlines] check box in the [*Windows*
Section] field. Choose [OK] when you've finished.

Turning gridlines back on

Follow the above procedure, but check the [Gridlines]
check box (i.e. click on it to insert a cross).

Colouring gridlines

You can also make gridlines display (and print, if you
have a colour printer) in colour. Make sure the
[Gridlines] check box in the [*Windows* Section] of the
[View] tab is checked. Click on the down-pointing
arrow to the right of the [Color] field. In the graphic
drop-down list which appears, select the colour you
want to use. Choose [OK] to confirm.

Checking spelling

Excel 5.0 for Windows comes with its own spelling
checker. Here's how to use it. To check the whole of a
worksheet, select any cell. Alternatively, to check a cell
range, highlight it.

You can also check multiple ranges in one operation. To
select multiple ranges, hold down one [Ctrl] key as you
highlight them in the normal way.

If the formula bar is active when you start its spelling
checker, by default *Excel* checks the entire contents of
the formula bar.

Pull down the [Tools] menu and choose [Spelling], or
click on the [Spelling] button in the overhead
[Standard] toolbar.

There's a keyboard short-cut here. Simply press [F7]
from within your worksheet.

Spelling
button

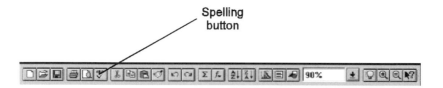

Checking begins immediately. If no misspelled words
are found, *Excel* simply produces a dialogue box
informing you that the operation has been completed
successfully.

Cells containing formulae are not checked.

If it encounters what it thinks is an error, *Excel*
launches the following:

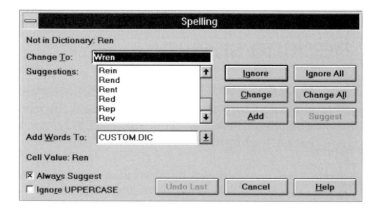

The message 'Not in Dictionary: xxxx' appears, where
[xxxx] is the disputed word. There are various options
here.

Change

If the [Always Suggest] box is ticked, *Excel* will provide
alternatives in the [Suggestions] box (if it can find
any).

If you need suggestions, and *Excel 5.0 for Windows* doesn't supply any, see 'Suggest' below.

One of these will be highlighted in the [Change To] field. To replace the incorrect word with the word in [Change To], click on [Change]. If the word in [Change To] isn't correct, scroll through the list of alternatives in [Suggestions]. If one of the suggestions is right, highlight it; the [Change To] field is updated accordingly. Click on [Change] so that *Excel* updates your worksheet.

Change All

[Change All] has the same effect as [Change], with one exception: it changes all instances of the incorrect word to the replacement you specify.

If *Excel* doesn't provide the correct alternative, you can edit the word directly in [Change To]. Simply click in [Change To] and make the necessary amendments.

Ignore

Choose [Ignore] to pass over the flagged word and continue checking.

Ignore All

Choose [Ignore All] so that *Excel* will ignore all occurrences of the word in the current worksheet.

If *Excel* encounters the same word while it's checking the spelling in another worksheet in the same workbook, it will still flag it (unless you've selected multiple sheets before starting the spelling check).

Add

Excel maintains two basic dictionaries. One, its main dictionary, can't be accessed by the user. The second dictionary, however, can. CUSTOM.DIC — your *Excel* user dictionary – is empty until you tell *Excel* to add words to it. Click on [Add] to add a highlighted word to CUSTOM.DIC.

You can create your own user dictionary. Click in [Add Words To]. Type in a name for the new dictionary and press ENTER.

Ignore UPPERCASE

This tells *Excel 5.0 for Windows* not to check the spelling of words consisting entirely of capital letters.

Undo Last

This tells *Excel* to revoke the last spelling change.

Cancel

Click here to terminate a spelling check before *Excel* has finished.

[Cancel] changes to [Close] when you've told *Excel* to insert a revised spelling. However, the button still serves the same purpose.

Workspaces

We looked at workbooks in Chapter 3. To recap here, workbooks consist of worksheets and charts, in any permutations (charts are discussed in Chapter 11). This is a useful technique for organising spreadsheet data. However, *Excel 5.0 for Windows* has another. You can organise your work into 'workspaces'.

Workspace

A workspace is a file which records the way multiple workbooks were arranged on your computer when you last closed *Excel 5.0 for Windows*. Information recorded in workspace files includes: workbook size, grouping, screen position.

The advantage is that, if an arrangement of workbooks is one you use frequently, you can load all the workbooks (organised in the most productive order) in one operation. *Excel* will even open the workspace file automatically, if you want.

Saving open workbooks as workspace files

Open those workbooks whose details you want to save in the workspace file (for details of how to do this, see 'Opening Existing Workbooks' in Chapter 3). Arrange them on screen in the way you want duplicated in the workspace file. Pull down the [File] menu and choose [Save Workspace].

In the [Save Workspace] dialogue, either:

1.   Accept the recommended file name: RESUME.XLW, or

2.   Type in one of your own, instead.

Choose [OK] to save the workspace.

Opening workspaces

Pull down the [File] menu and choose [Open]. The [Open] dialogue launches.

Click on the down-pointing arrow to the right of the [List Files of Type] field. In the list which appears, select [Workspaces (*.xlw)]. The [File Name] list displays all workspace files stored in the current directory (if you need to switch to another directory, use the [Directories] box to move through your directory tree). Highlight the workspace file you want open in the [File Name] list and click on [OK].

Automatic workspace loading

Follow the procedure set out in 'Saving Open Workbooks as Workspace Files', with one difference. Save your workbook arrangement as a workspace in your D:\EXCEL\XLSTART directory, where [D] is the drive on which *Excel* is installed.

Organising worksheets

You can refine your worksheet by naming cells; using the Outline feature; adding cell notes; and hiding/unhiding data. If you make errors in the process, you can Undo them! Even better – Repeat lets you duplicate actions that *aren't* wrong.

7

Organising worksheets

Names

To illustrate the use of names, we'll use our sample worksheet again. Load up the worksheet in the usual way. Wouldn't it be handy if we could allocate names to the Deposit and Withdrawal totals (D40 and E40)? This would enable us to redefine D43.

Naming cells

Naming cells won't actually help us much in our Transaction Inventory spreadsheet, because it's reasonably simple. However, once you start defining larger and more complex worksheets you'll find this feature invaluable.

Let's rename D40. Make sure D40 is selected. Pull down the [Insert] menu and choose [Name], [Define]. Alternatively, press [Ctrl]-[F3].

In the [Define Name] dialogue, type in the name you want to allocate in the [Names in Workbook] field. In this case, type in [Deposits] and click on [OK].

Allocated names

Excel lists names which have already been allocated in the [Names in Workbook] list. If you want to allocate one of these, highlight it. Note, however, that the new name definition replaces the old.

If the cell or cell ranges selected prior to defining a name contain text (or are to the right of or below a text entry), this appears in the [Names in Workbook] list.

Permissible names

Names can be up to 255 characters long, in any permutation of upper and lower case. As well as letters, they can also contain:

- Numerals [0 to 9]
- Underline characters [_]
- Backslashes [\]
- Full stops [.]
- Question marks [?]

However, the first character must be a letter, an underline or a backslash, and names are not allowed to resemble numbers or cell references.

You can use the Name box to the left of the Formula Bar to apply names (see the 'Name Box' section in Chapter 3 for information on how to do this).

Repeat the above process for E40, but allocate this name: `Withdrawals`.

Substituting names in formulae

Excel provides a very useful short-cut for transposing names into formulae. Look at the next illustration.

Select D43 (note that, because these cells have had a border imposed earlier in this book, *Excel* indicates that D43 has been selected by de-emphasising it). The Formula Bar displays the formula associated with D43: D40-E40. We could, of course, physically amend this cell reference to:

`Deposits-Withdrawals`

but with a larger formula this process would be tedious, and error-prone. Here's how to do it much more easily. Select the cell or range of cells you want to work with (in this case, D43). Pull down the [Insert] menu and choose [Name], [Apply]. The [Apply Names] dialogue launches.

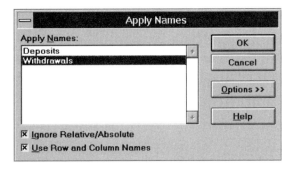

Excel has inserted the new cell names into the [Apply Names] box. Select each name, and click on [OK] so that *Excel* substitutes them into the formula.

Pasting names into the Formula Bar

Excel lets you insert names into the Formula Bar on-the-fly. Here's how to do this.

Activate the Formula Bar by clicking in it. Type [=], to begin the formula. Pull down the [Insert] menu and choose [Name], [Paste]. Or press [F3] instead. In the [Paste Name] dialogue, highlight one of the listed names. Choose [OK] to insert it into the Formula Bar.

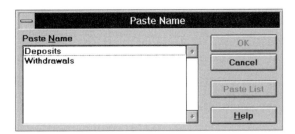

Pasting when Formula Bar isn't active

Pull down the [Insert] menu and choose [Name],
[Paste]. Or press [F3] instead. In the [Paste Name]
dialogue, highlight one of the listed names. Choose
[OK]; *Excel* activates the Formula Bar automatically
and inserts the highlighted name prefixed by [=].

Deleting names

You can use the [Define Name] dialogue to delete
names. Pull down the [Insert] menu and choose
[Name], [Define]. In the [Names in Workbook] list in
the [Define Name] dialogue, highlight the name you
want to erase and click on the [Delete] button. Choose
[OK].

Names in formulae

When you delete names which are present in formulae,
Excel replaces all occurrences of the formula with an
error value. For instance, if in our sample worksheet
we deleted [Deposit] in the [Define Name] dialogue,
D43 would return the following:

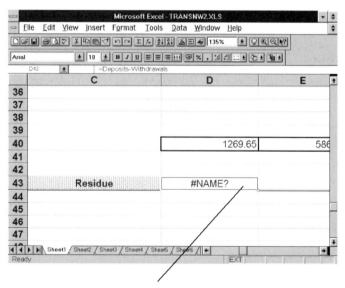

Excel displays an error message

There is a way to avoid this. Before you delete the name, do the following:

1. Pull down the [Edit] menu and choose [Replace].

2. In the [Replace] dialogue, enter [Deposits] in the [Find What] field.

3. In the [Replace With] field, type in the formula definition. In this case, SUM(D6:D39)

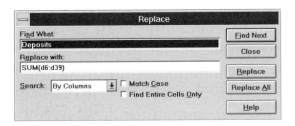

Click on [Replace All] to substitute the definition for the name. Now carry out the name deletion as above. (See Chapter 12 for more information on *Excel's* Find and Replace features).

Using names and Go To

We looked at the [Go To] feature in 'Using Go To' in Chapter 4. (See also 'Selecting Specific Cell Types' in Chapter 5). You can use [Go To] to jump to cells with specific names. Press [F5]; *Excel* lists the assigned names in the [Go To] field. To move to a name, highlight it and choose [OK].

Outlining

Outlining – the ability to determine which levels in a document will be displayed – is common to most word processors now. *Excel* adds this feature to its worksheets. The advantage of applying outlines is that it enables you to achieve an overview at the click of a mouse.

Applying outlines to worksheets doesn't change the data in any way; it merely determines which sections of it you see at any given time.

You can apply outlines to worksheets which are organised into rows or columns with totals or sub-totals.

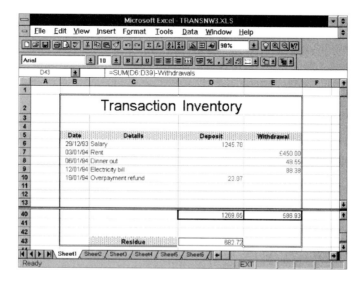

Splitting windows

This illustration shows two views of the same worksheet. In the top view, we see the main heading and data; in the lower view, the totals. To achieve this, place the cursor in the row in which you want the split to take effect. Pull down the [Window] menu and choose [Split].

Excel splits the screen. To adjust the split, move the mouse pointer over the horizontal or vertical boundaries. Click and drag them to the new location. Release the mouse button to confirm. Note that in the earlier illustration, the vertical divider has been moved to the left margin for easier viewing. To remove

the split, pull down the [Window] menu again and
choose [Remove Split].

To ensure that one 'pane' is unaltered, make sure it's
active and then pull down the [Window] menu. Choose
[Freeze Panes].

This worksheet has totals, and is therefore a suitable
candidate for outlining:

1. Click in one cell in the worksheet you want to
outline (or select the appropriate cell ranges if you want
to limit the outline to these).

2. Pull down the [Data] menu and select [Group and
Outline], [Auto Outline].

Excel applies the necessary outline to the worksheet
(you'd repeat this procedure for subordinate rows or
columns, if there were any). This is the result.

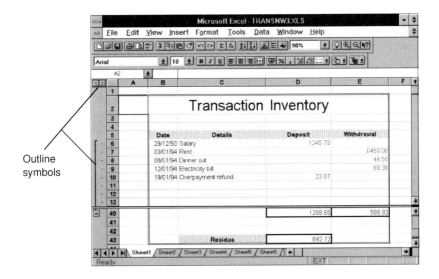

Outline
symbols

The only visible change – until you invoke the Outline
feature – is the presence of Outline symbols on the left
of the screen.

Determining which levels display

Click on one of the number buttons which *Excel* inserts.

The higher the number, the more detail displays.

Clicking on [1] produces the following result.

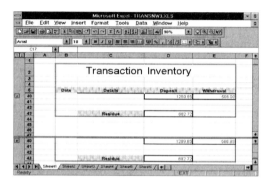

Excel has hidden the data; only the headings and totals display. If you click on [2], because there are only two levels in this sheet *Excel* displays the whole of the sheet.

You can also click on the [+] and [-] buttons in the Outline symbols area. [+] expands the outline by one level; [-] contracts it.

[Auto Outline] automates the entire process. However, on occasion it may not outline a worksheet correctly. If it doesn't, you can rectify this by 'regrouping' ranges as outline levels.

Grouping and ungrouping

Grouping

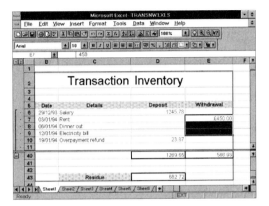

Cells E7:E10 have been selected. If you wanted to group these cells as a level in their own right, you'd do the following. Pull down the [Data] menu and choose [Group and Outline], [Group]. This is the result:

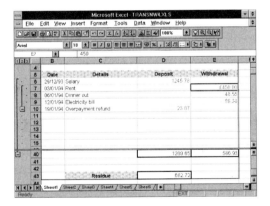

Excel has inserted an extra level: [3], and an additional [-]. Clicking on [2] now will display all data in the worksheet except for the grouped cells (clicking on the new [-] produces the same result).

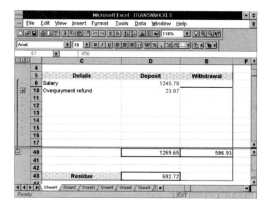

Ungrouping

First ensure the grouped cells are displayed by clicking on the relevant Outline level number – in this case, [3]. See earlier for how to do this. Select the relevant cell range. Pull down the [Data] menu and choose [Group and Outline], [Ungroup].

You can 'undo' the grouping if you've only just implemented it. See 'Undo and Repeat' below.

Removing the outline

To stop viewing a worksheet as an outline, do the following: Pull down the [Data] menu and choose [Group and Outline], [Clear Outline].

Undo and Repeat

Excel lets you reverse many (but not all) editing commands, or erase typing. You can also repeat the last command.

Undo

You can only undo one level of editing actions or typing, i.e. you can only do so providing no other actions have been taken in the interim. And you can only repeat the very last command.

Undo

Pull down the [Edit] menu and select [Undo]. This provides details of the action to be reversed. For instance, if you've just typed in text or numbers and want to remove them, the relevant [Edit] menu command is: [Undo Entry]. If the editing action can't be undone (for instance, *Excel's* Auto Outline feature – see above), the [Edit] menu tells you.

Immediately after you undo an action, the [Edit] menu command changes to [Redo...]. This lets you undo the undo.

There are two keyboard short-cuts for [Undo]. Press: [Ctrl]-[Z], or [Alt]-BACKSPACE.

You can also launch Undo from the [Standard] toolbar. Simply click on the [Undo] button.

Undo
button

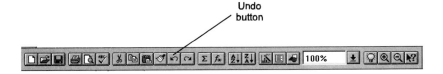

Repeat

To repeat the last action, pull down the [Edit] menu and choose [Repeat]. Alternatively, press [F4], or [Alt]-RETURN. Note that *Excel* provides details of the action to be repeated. If the editing action can't be repeated, the [Edit] menu says: [Can't Repeat].

The [Repeat] command is effective across workbooks. For instance, if you carry out one action in one workbook, you can switch to another workbook and initiate it again by selecting [Repeat].

Cell notes

Excel lets you insert notes into cells. This is useful if your worksheets are shared with other users. Even if they're not, you can still insert explanatory notes. For instance, you can insert text into a cell clarifying the associated formula. You can use notes to indicate how the worksheet is set up.

Adding notes

Select the cell into which you want to insert the note. Pull down the [Insert] menu and choose [Note], or press SHIFT-[F2]. The [Cell Note] dialogue appears.

The cursor is automatically positioned in the [Text Note] section. Begin to type in the note.

Text notes

You can use standard Microsoft *Windows* copy-and-paste and cut-and-paste techniques here (see 'Amending the Contents of Existing Cells' in Chapter 4). And the contents of the [Text Note] field are automatically subject to word wrap (for a practical definition of 'word wrap', see 'Applying Text Wrap' in Chapter 6).

A practical example

In the last illustration, cell C10 in our sample worksheet has been selected; we're going to insert a useful note. Type the following into the [Text Notes] field:
Should the repayment be more? Check this!

Click on [Add]; the text you've typed in appears in the [Notes in Sheet] field. It's also added to the cell.

Using the Cell Note dialogue

Cell Note dialogue

After you've clicked on [Add], you can use the [Cell Note] dialogue to add notes to additional cells, without having to close and reopen the dialogue. Simply click on the relevant cell within the worksheet. *Excel* surrounds the cell with a dotted, moving frame.

Now click in the [Text Note] field and type in a new note, or edit the original, if appropriate.

When you've finished with the [Cell Note] dialogue, choose [OK]. To show that a cell contains a note, *Excel* inserts a small red bullet into the upper right-hand corner.

Amending existing notes

Select the cell whose note you want to revise. Launch the [Cell Note] dialogue, as above. The associated note is highlighted in the [Notes in Sheet] field, and its text displays in the [Text Note] box.

Instead of selecting the relevant cell first, you can launch the [Cell Note] dialogue directly. Choose the note you want to revise in the [Notes in Sheet] field.

Amend or add to the note in the [Text Note] field, as required. Choose [OK] when you've finished.

Deleting notes

While the [Cell Note] dialogue is open, you can delete notes. Highlight the note you want to erase in the [Notes in Sheet] field. Click on the [Delete] button. A message appears, warning you that the deletion is irreversible. Choose [OK] to proceed.

Deletion is irreversible.

Copying notes

Excel has special techniques for copying notes from one cell to another (see 'Amending the Contents of Existing Cells' in Chapter 4).

1.   Select the cell (or cell range) whose notes you want to copy.

2.   Pull down the [Edit] menu and select [Copy]. *Excel* surrounds the selection with a moving frame.

3.   Select the cell you want to copy the notes to (or the top left corner of the range you want to copy the notes to).

4.   Pull down the [Edit] menu and select [Paste Special].

5.   In the [Paste Special] dialogue, choose [Notes].

Click on [OK] to confirm the operation.

Copying cell contents

1.   If you want to copy all the contents of a cell, including notes, choose [All] instead of [Notes] in step 5. Alternatively, choose [Paste] in step 4 instead of [Paste Special] and omit step 5.

2.   See Chapter 8 for how to print notes.

Hiding data

Excel lets you conceal the following worksheet components:

* Formulae in cells
* Rows/columns

You can also hide worksheets and workbooks.

Hiding cell formulae

This is a two stage process.

Stage 1: Hiding the cell

Select the cell – or cell range – whose formulae you wish to hide. Pull down the [Format] menu and choose [Cells]. In the [Format Cells] dialogue, click on the [Protection] tab.

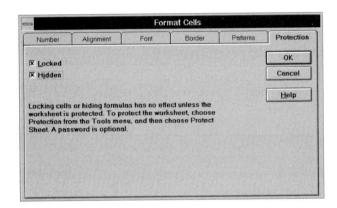

Check the [Hidden] box, and click on [OK].

Locked cells

By default, all *Excel* cells are 'locked'. When cells are locked – but only after stage 2 below has been carried out – no changes to cell contents are permissible (and otherwise active menu components which are no longer applicable are greyed out).

Stage 2: Protecting the worksheet

Pull down the [Tools] menu and select [Protection], [Protect Sheet]. The [Protect Sheet] dialogue launches. Make sure the [Contents] box is checked.

Click on [OK]. If you've applied a password in the [Password (Optional)] field, *Excel* produces the [Confirm Password] dialogue. Type in the password again and click on [OK].

Remember that if you lose your password, there is no way to bypass it. Keep a copy of it in a safe place.

Although a formula may be hidden, the number currently returned by the formula will still be displayed.

Unhiding cell formulae

You can 'unhide' cell contents by removing worksheet
protection. Select the sheet whose protection you want
to rescind. Pull down the [Tools] menu and select
[Protection], [Unprotect Sheet]. If you allocated a
password in Stage 2, the [Unprotect Sheet] dialogue
appears. Type in the password and choose [OK].

Hiding rows/columns

You can hide rows and columns, and re-display them
again just as easily. You can hide rows and columns by:

1. Using a menu route

2. Using the mouse

Hiding rows

First, the menu route:

1. Select the row (or rows) you want to hide (for
multiple row selection techniques, see 'Selecting
Multiple Rows or Columns' in Chapter 5).

2. Pull down the [Format] menu and choose [Row],
[Hide].

There's a keyboard short-cut here. Press [Ctrl]-[9]
instead of Step 2.

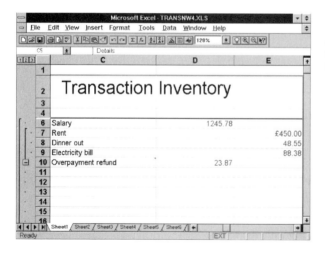

*The sample worksheet.
Row 5 (it contains the
column sub-headings)
has been hidden.*

All You Need To Know About
                                Excel 5.0 for Windows

Now the mouse route. Move the mouse pointer over the row heading. More specifically, position it over the lower row edge. The cursor becomes a black cross.

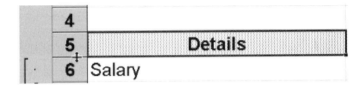

Drag the lower border up until it's flush with the higher. The row 'disappears'.

Unhiding rows

Again, there are two routes.

Using menus

Select the rows immediately above and below the hidden row (for instance, to re-display row 5, select rows 4 and 6). Pull down the [Format] menu and choose [Row], [Unhide].

Unhide

For some reason, the menu unhide route only works on rows which have been hidden using the menu route (see steps 1 and 2 above). To unhide rows hidden using the mouse, see 'Using the Mouse' below.

Using the mouse

Place the mouse pointer between the row headings immediately above and below the hidden row (for example, to unhide row 5 position the pointer equidistant between rows 4 and 6). Move the pointer slightly until the horizontal component of the black cross changes from a single into a double line. Drag the row border down.

The keyboard short-cut here is: [Ctrl]-SHIFT-[9].

Hiding columns

The menu route:

1. Select the column (or columns) you want to hide (for multiple column selection techniques, see 'Selecting Multiple Rows or Columns' in Chapter 5).

2. Pull down the [Format] menu and choose [Column], [Hide].

 There's a keyboard short-cut here too. Press [Ctrl]-[0] (zero) instead of Step 2.

The mouse route:

Position the mouse cursor over the right column edge in the column heading. It changes into a black cross.

Drag the right border over the left. The next illustration shows our sample worksheet with column C hidden.

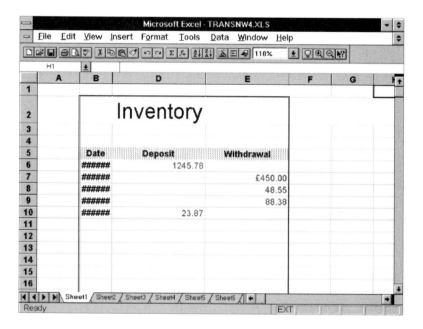

Unhiding columns

Once more, there are menu and mouse routes.

Using menus to re-display columns

Select the columns immediately to the left and right of the hidden column (for instance, to re-display column C, select columns B and D). Pull down the [Format] menu and choose [Column], [Unhide].

Using the mouse

Place the mouse pointer between the column headings immediately to the left and right of the hidden column (for example, to unhide column C, position the pointer equidistant between columns B and D). Move the pointer slightly until the vertical component of the black cross changes from a single- into a double-line. Drag the column border to the right.

The keyboard short-cut here is: [Ctrl]-SHIFT- [O] (zero).

Hiding worksheets

It can sometimes be useful to hide worksheets. Hiding worksheets can only be accomplished through the use of menus. Another proviso is that the workbook whose sheet you want to hide must contain more than one.

Here's how to hide worksheets.

1. Select the sheet you want to hide (by clicking on the relevant sheet tab). You can select more than one sheet if you want (by holding down [Ctrl] as you click on the tabs).

2. Pull down the [Format] menu and select [Sheet], [Hide].

This is the result when sheets 1, 5 and 6 in our sample worksheet have been hidden.

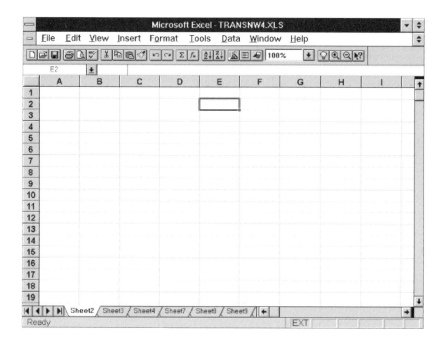

The sheet tabs at the base of the screen show the
effects.

Unhiding single worksheets

Pull down the [Format] menu and select [Sheet],
[Unhide]. The [Unhide] dialogue appears. Highlight
the sheet you want to re-display. Press [OK] to confirm.

 You can only unhide worksheets singly. You can't select
more than one at a time in the [Unhide] dialogue.

Hiding workbooks

You can also hide entire workbooks. Here's how to do
this.

Open the workbook you want to hide. (See 'Opening
Existing Workbooks' in Chapter 3 for more

information on how to do this.) Pull down the [Window] menu and choose [Hide].

Unhiding workbooks

Pull down the [Window] menu and choose [Unhide].

Unhide

If the workbook you've hidden was the only one currently open, you need to follow a different route to re-display it. Pull down the [File] menu and choose [Unhide].

8

Printing

When you need to print out your worksheets, you can preview them first. You can also use Preview to adjust printable margins and control the layout of printed worksheets. If you don't need to use Preview, you can determine all this anyway directly from within a worksheet.

All You Need To Know About
Excel 5.0 for Windows

Printing

Print preview

Print Preview is a useful tool. Use it to proof
worksheets before you print them out. Print Preview
lets you determine how each page of an active
worksheet will look when printed.

Activating print preview

Print Preview
button

Pull down the [File] menu and choose [Print Preview].
Alternatively, click on the [Print Preview] button on
the [Standard] toolbar.

 Holding down one SHIFT key while you click on the
[Print Preview] button produces a different effect: it
makes it function like the [Print] button (see 'Printing'
below).

The next illustration shows our sample worksheet in
Print Preview mode.

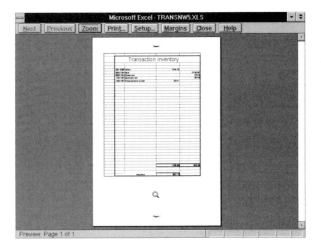

Notice that the mouse pointer becomes a magnifying glass when positioned over the page area. This is part of *Excel*'s Zoom feature; see 'Zoom' below.

By default, the [Print Preview] window shows your worksheet in full-page view. You can easily change this. You can also implement additional features by clicking on the buttons across the top of the screen.

Next & previous

Click on [Next] to move to the next page. Click on [Previous] to show the preceding page.

Zoom

Click on the [Zoom] button to view your document with a higher level of magnification. Use the horizontal and vertical scroll bars (or the cursor keys) to move through the preview. When full-page view is in force, the scroll bars and cursor keys move you through successive pages.

The *Excel* [Zoom] feature has no impact on printing size: it's only there to allow you to inspect your work.

Zoom

To save time, do the following. Move the mouse pointer (shown as a magnifying glass) over the section of the page area you want to 'zoom in' on and click to expand it. Click again to return to full-page view.

Refer to the status bar at the bottom of the screen for details of:

1. The current page number

2. The total number of pages in the worksheet

Print Preview on your computer may not look quite like the earlier illustrations. This is because *Excel* bases the way your worksheet looks on the following variables:

- The typefaces installed on your system

- Your printer's resolution in dots-per-inch (dpi)

- The number of colours your Microsoft *Windows* display driver/card supports

Excel lets you pre-select the pages you want to preview. Here's how to do this:

Pre-select for preview

Pull down the [File] menu and choose [Print]. Alternatively, press [Ctrl]-[P]. Click in the [From] box in the [Print] dialogue.

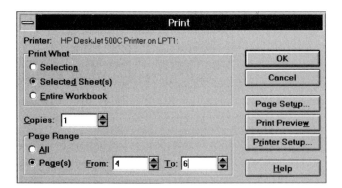

Insert the number of the first page you want to preview. Click in the [To] box and type in the last page number. Click on the [Print Preview] button. (For more information on the use of the [Print] dialogue, see 'Printing' below).

The *Excel 5.0 for Windows* [Zoom] feature has no impact on printing size: it's only there to allow you to inspect your work.

For information on printing charts, see Chapter 11.

Print

Click on [Print] to produce the [Print] dialogue (for more information on how to use this, see 'Printing' below). Note that if you used the [Print] dialogue initially to select the appropriate page range to preview, clicking on [Print] within Print Preview mode prints the previewed pages.

Setup

Click on [Setup] to produce the [Page Setup] dialogue (see 'Page Setup' below for how to use this).

Margins

Click on [Margins] for margin lines and handles. You can use these to adjust top, bottom, left and right page margins. When you do so, *Excel* displays the new item dimensions in the status bar in the bottom left hand corner of the screen.

Note that the dimensions are only displayed for as long as the mouse button is depressed, and for this reason are omitted from the illustration on the next page.

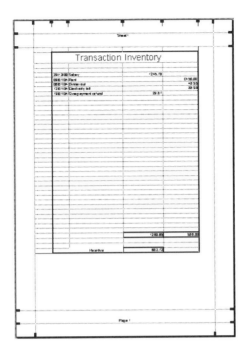

Position the mouse pointer over one of the lines or a handle; it changes to a black cross. Click and hold with the left mouse button. Drag the line to its new location. Release the button to confirm the move.

If you're previewing a worksheet, *Excel* also inserts lines which correspond to columns; if you need to adjust column dimensions, you can do so by dragging the lines.

Printer drivers

The margins which *Excel* can implement depend on your printer driver. For example, some printer drivers don't support printing on the edge of a page. If your printer falls into this category, *Excel* will prevent you from moving the handles/lines to an area which won't print.

To return to the standard Print Preview screen without margin and column lines, click on the [Margins] button again. For more information on margins, see 'Page Margins' below.

Close

To shut down Print Preview mode, click on the [Close button]; this returns you to your active worksheet. Alternatively, press [Esc].

Printing

Excel lets you print specific worksheet data, the active sheet, selected sheets or the whole of a workbook. Here's how to do this:

1. Open the appropriate workbook. (If you aren't sure how to do this, see 'Opening Existing Workbooks' in Chapter 3).

2. Do whichever of the following is most relevant:

- Select a specific cell range
- Select a specific worksheet by clicking on its tab
- Select more than one worksheet by holding down [Ctrl] as you click on their tabs

3. Pull down the [File] menu and select [Print].

The [Print] dialogue which launches provides a wealth of options. You can:

- Choose [Selection] in the [Print What] section (if you chose [a.] above)
- Choose [Selected Sheets] in the [Print What] section if you chose [b.] or [c.] above
- Choose [Entire Workbook] in the [Print What] section to print the whole workbook

The [Print What] section is an alternative to the [Print Area] field in the [Page Setup] dialogue; see 'The Sheet Tab' later for more information.

Printing more than one copy

To print multiple copies, click within the [Copies] field. Type in the number of copies you require.

Printing page ranges

If you don't need to print the whole of a worksheet, click in the [From] field and enter the page number from which you want printing to begin. Click in the [To] field and enter the finishing page number.

Page Setup

The [Page Setup] button provides access to features which control the layout of the worksheets you print.

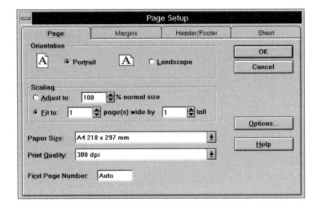

You can also reach the [Page Setup] dialogue via the following route.

Page Setup

Pull down the [File] menu and select [Page Setup]. The dialogue is slightly different if you invoke it in this way. For instance, the [Page] tab has a [Print] button which launches the [Print] dialogue.

As with many *Excel* dialogues, the [Page Setup] dialogue consists of a number of tabs:

The Page tab

Click on the [Page] tab if it isn't already active. Features in this tab control general page layout and print quality.

Print orientation

Choose [Portrait] to have your work printed from the
top to the bottom of the page. Choose [Landscape] to
print it out sideways.

Scaling

Click in the [Adjust To] text entry box and enter a
percentage less than [100%] so that *Excel* reduces the
size of the printout. A figure in excess of [100%]
produces a larger printout. Alternatively, click on [Fit
To] and enter the appropriate page numbers in the two
text entry boxes on the right to scale the document
accordingly.

Paper size

Click on the down-pointing arrow to the right of the
[Paper Size] field. In the list which appears, select the
appropriate page size.

Print quality

The options *Excel 5.0 for Windows* provides here
depend on the printer you have installed. For instance,
Excel offers High, Medium, Low and Draft for many
printers. On the other hand, many ink-jet users will
find themselves limited to a single resolution,
expressed in dpi.

 Dpi (or 'Dots per Inch) is one of the main ways of
measuring the resolution of printed output. The higher
the number, the better the print quality.

Click on the down-pointing arrow to the right of [Print
Quality] and select the correct option from the list.

Page numbering

By default, *Excel 5.0 for Windows* prints page numbers
in the footer area (see 'Header/Footer Margins' later).
Also by default, *Excel* starts numbering at [1]. If you
want to start from a different number, click in the text
entry box to the right of [First Page Number] and type
it in.

Options

> This button (it's repeated in all the tabs) provides access to Printer Setup options; see 'Options' later.

The Margins tab

> Click on the [Margins] tab if it isn't already active. This tab controls page and header/footer margins.

Page margins

> To adjust the top, bottom, left or right page margins, click in any of the [Top], [Bottom], [Left] and [Right] text entry fields and enter the appropriate figure.

Header/footer margins

> To adjust the header or footer margins, click in the [Header] or [Footer] text entry boxes and enter the appropriate figure.

Headers and footers

Headers consist of text repeated identically at the top of each page of a worksheet. Footers are repeated at the bottom of each page. Headers and footers often consist of page numbers, worksheet titles, date, origination details.

Adjusting the page positioning

> You can elect to have your worksheet centred on the printable page, horizontally and/or vertically. Choose both [Horizontal] and [Vertical] to print your document in the very centre.

All changes you make to margins are reflected in the [Preview] window. Use this to see how the amendments look before you confirm them.

The Header/Footer tab

> Click on the [Header/Footer]] tab if it isn't already active. *Excel* offers two basic choices. You can either make use of a variety of pre-defined headers and footers, or you can create your own.

Using preset headers/footers

To implement a header, click on the down-pointing
arrow to the right of the [Header] field.

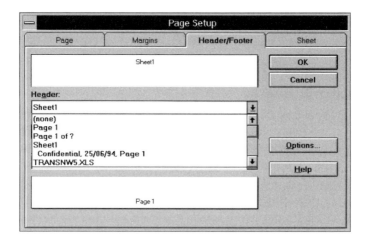

To utilise a footer, click on the arrow to the right of the
[Footer] field. Choose the text you want to use by
clicking on it.

Commas

The commas which separate entries split them into
areas. Text on the left of the first comma appears on the
left of the header or footer. Text on the immediate left
of the middle comma displays in the centre. Text before
the final comma appears on the right.

Customising headers/footers

To create your own header format, click on the [Custom
Header] button. To create your own footer, click on the
[Custom Footer] button. The next illustration shows
the [Footer] dialogue; the [Header] dialogue is almost
identical.

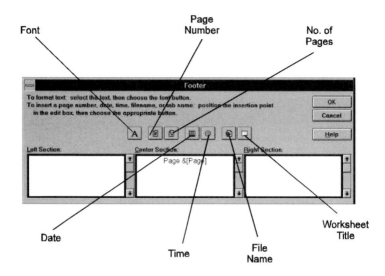

Enter text, as appropriate, into the [Left Section],
[Center Section] and [Right Section] fields.

Inserting special text

With the insertion point positioned in the relevant
field, click on any of the special buttons (see the
illustration above). *Excel* inserts codes automatically
for: page numbers; total number of pages; current
date; current time; file name; worksheet title.

Formatting text

You can apply standard *Excel* text formatting to the
header and footer text you enter. Here's how to do this.
Select the text first in the normal way. Then click on
the [Font] button. A special form of the [Font] dialogue
launches.

This is almost identical to the standard [Font]
dialogue; the difference is that you can't change the
colour of header/footer. Make any typeface/type size
changes which are required. (See 'Inserting the
Heading' in Chapter 4 for how to complete this
dialogue). Click on [OK] when you're ready.

When you've finished creating your own header or
footer, choose [OK] to return to the [Header/Footer] tab
of the [Page Setup] dialogue.

The Sheet tab

Click on the [Sheet] tab if it isn't already active.

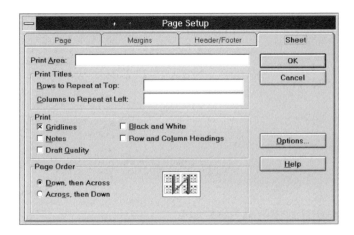

Use the [Sheet] tab to exercise control over a variety of
print features, including:

- Which sections of the worksheet are printed
- Whether titles are printed
- Whether gridlines are printed
- Whether hidden notes are printed
- Whether column/row headings are printed

Print area

If you want to print a specific cell range, enter the
reference in the [Print Area] field. For instance,
[C2:F34,H15:L22] would print the range whose top left
and bottom right cell components were C2 and F34
respectively, and also the range whose coordinates
were H15 and L22. Multiple ranges print out on
separate pages if they're not contiguous.

Use this technique if you regularly want to print a specific area. If you want to print varying areas, however, use the [Print What] section in the [Print] dialogue; see 'Printing' earlier for how to do this.

You can also use the mouse to select the cell range you want to print.

Click in the [Print Area] field. Now move the mouse pointer outside the dialogue and select the cells you want to print. You may have to move the dialogue to do so (for how to do this, see 'Moving Windows' – 'The Mouse Route' in Chapter 2). *Excel 5.0 for Windows* surrounds them with a moving dashed line and updates the [Print Area] accordingly.

Print titles

You can specify row or column data as print titles. Here's how to do this.

Click in the [Rows To Repeat At Top] field to select row data as a title. Or click in the [Columns To Repeat At Left] field to select column information. Then move the mouse pointer into the worksheet itself and click on the row or dialogue, as appropriate.

You can also enter the row or column coordinates directly into the [Rows To Repeat At Top] and [Columns To Repeat At Left] fields.

If you select a row or column as a print title, *Excel* must print out the original row or column first. It's only after this that the selected data prints as a title.

Print

Select any of the following options in the [Print] section:

[Gridlines]
Prints horizontal and vertical worksheet gridlines (this is selected by default)

[Notes]
Prints cell notes on additional pages

[Draft Quality]
Most graphics images don't print (this option also turns off grid line printing). Printing times are reduced.

[Black And White]
Prints in black and white. This is recommended for black and white printing on a colour printer: it speeds up the process.

[Row And Column Headings]
Prints row numbers and column references.

Page order

If the information you want to print won't fit on a single page, you can specify how *Excel* should paginate it.

Choose either [Down, Then Across] or [Across, Then Down]. To see the effect each option has, look at the small preview to the right of the [Page Order] section.

Options

Click here to adjust your printer settings.

When you choose this option, *Excel* produces a dialogue which is specific to your active printer driver. Typically, you'll be able to adjust:

* Paper size
* Print quality/resolution
* Orientation (landscape/portrait)
* Paper source
* Number of copies

Refer to your system documentation for additional clarification.

When you've finished with the [Page Setup] dialogue, click on [OK] to return to the [Print] dialogue. For information on how to complete this, see 'Printing' earlier.

9

More on functions

Discover some more of the advanced features of *Excel*. You can insert them directly, or use Function Wizard to automate the process. You'll also work with arrays, advanced series, trends and links. Sounds complex? It isn't.

More on functions

In this chapter, we look at:

- Using functions
- Using Function Wizard
- Arrays
- Series / Trends
- Links

Functions

So far, we've discussed a few of the more frequently used functions in passing (see Chapter 5). These have included the following arithmetical functions:

[+]

[-]

[/]

[*]

We've also worked with SUM.

Function

A function is a preset tool with a specific name which produces a certain result. The result can be a calculation, or a more generalised operation, and a common facet to all functions is that they replace a number of formulae. For example, SUM totals a series of cell values; without this, you'd have to add each number separately.

Functions can only be used in formulae.

Now let's look at functions in greater detail. *Excel* has a large number of functions, in several broad categories. For instance, there are:

- Mathematical functions
- Engineering functions
- Statistical functions
- Financial functions
- Text functions
- Date and Time functions

For details of individual functions, see *Excel's* on-line help.

There are two ways to enter functions. You can type them directly into cells, or you can use Function Wizard.

Wizards

Wizards are interactive aids which lead you through specific tasks. *Excel 5.0 for Windows* incorporates several wizards. These are discussed in more detail in Chapter 13.

Using Function Wizard

1. Select the cell into which you want to insert a function.

2. Pull down the [Insert] menu and choose [Function].

Alternatively, perform [1.]. Press [F2] or click in the Formula Bar. Click on the [Function Wizard] button next to the Formula Bar.

There's a keyboard route, too. Press SHIFT-[F3].

Function Wizard button

All You Need To Know About
Excel 5.0 for Windows

Step 1

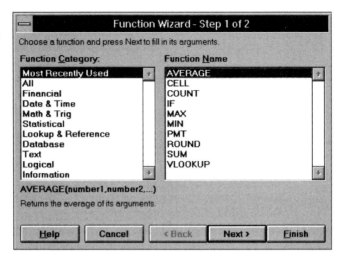

Function Wizard organises its functions under overall headings. Scroll through the categories in the [Function Category] field until you highlight the right one. As you do so, the [Function Name] field lists associated functions. Beneath the [Function Category] field, *Excel* inserts brief details of what each function does.

When you've highlighted the function you want to use in the [Function Name] box, click on [Next] to enter the next stage of the process.

Step 2 of Function Wizard looks like this.

Step 2

This dialogue box is organised in terms of function arguments.

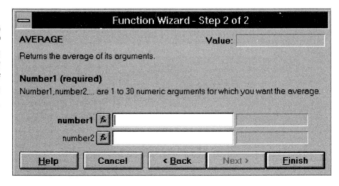

Arguments are the values on which functions act. Arguments are flexible. For instance, they can be numbers, names, other functions, or cell references.

Each argument which is appropriate to the function you've selected has its own text entry box (although they may not all be visible at the same time).

At the top of the [Step 2] dialogue, *Excel* lists the function title. On the right of this is the [Value] field; here, *Excel* displays the result of the arguments you enter. Below these is a section which provides brief details of the type of information required in the selected argument box.

In the case of the function we've chosen – AVERAGE – Function Wizard tells you that up to 30 numeric arguments can be entered. Click in the first text box. Enter a number. Press TAB to move to the next argument field; as you do so, *Excel 5.0 for Windows* adds another argument to the dialogue.

Enter as many numbers as you need.

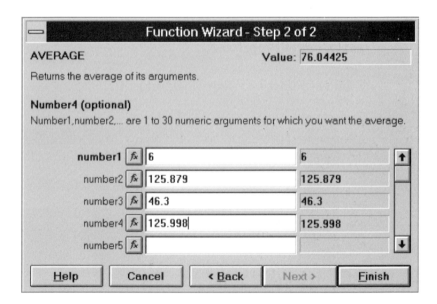

Notice that *Excel* has applied the selected function to
the inserted arguments; the result is displayed in the
[Value] field. When you've finished defining the
necessary arguments, click on [Finish].

Inserting functions directly

1. Select the cell into which you want to insert a
function.

2. Press [=] to activate the Formula Bar.

3. Type in the following, in this order: the function
name (the necessary arguments).

You can also bypass step 2. Perform step 1. Click in the
Formula Bar and enter the function directly into the
Formula Bar.

When you've finished typing in the function, press
ENTER or click on the Enter box next to the Formula
Bar.

**Mix &
match**

If you want, you can use a 'mix and match' approach.
Follow steps 1 and 2. Then press [Ctrl]-[A] to invoke
step 2 of the Function Wizard. Now proceed as per
'Step 2' above.

Function errors

If you enter a function manually and it's incorrect,
Excel puts up an 'Error in formula' message.
Correcting inaccurate formulae is sometimes easy.
For instance, if you entered:

AVERAGE (F12:L54)

in a selected cell, *Excel* would tell you it was wrong by
inserting [#NAME?]. One glance at the formula within
the host cell would be enough to spot the incorrect
space between the function and argument.

Excel corrects some errors automatically. For example, if you omit the final parenthesis in a function, it will insert it for you.

Other errors, however, are harder to isolate. The good news is that *Excel 5.0 for Windows* lets you use Function Wizard to 'debug' functions. Here's how to do this. Select the problem cell. Then click in the Formula Bar. Click on the [Function Wizard] button in the Formula Bar. Now use Function Wizard to restate the formula from scratch (see 'Using Function Wizard' earlier for how to do this).

Arrays

Arrays are a very useful component of *Excel 5.0 for Windows* formulae.

An array is simply a row or column of numbers.

Excel lets you use array formulae. The difference between array and normal formulae is that array formulae perform multiple calculations over more than one row or column. You can also use them to enter the same formula into multiple cells within a range.

Here's a simple illustration of an array formula. If you wanted to multiply the contents of F10 by the contents of G10, the standard formula =F10*G10 would give a single result. The following array formula, however:

`{ = (F10:F15) * (G10:G15) }`

would produce a set of six results:

    The result of multiplying F10 by G10
    The result of multiplying F11 by G11
    The result of multiplying F12 by G12
    The result of multiplying F13 by G13
    The result of multiplying F14 by G14
    The result of multiplying F15 by G16

For a visual exploration of this example, see 'Using Array Formulae for Interpolation' later.

Using array formulae for multiple calculations

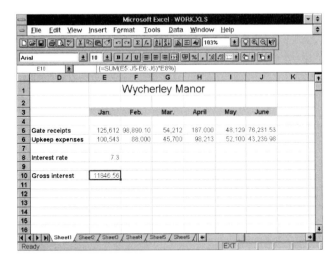

This simple worksheet calculates gross interest on net receipts for a fictitious country house. Row 5 lists income for a six month period. Row 6 lists outgoings. Cell E8 contains a figure for the applicable interest rate. E10 holds an array formula.

We need *Excel 5.0 for Windows* to total E5:J5, then total E6:J6. It then needs to subtract the second total from the first, to give the net receipts. This total should then be multiplied by the figure in E8 as a percentage. The result is the gross interest.

We could show this formula in full, if we wanted to:

`=SUM(E5+F5+G5+H5+I5+J5-E6-F6-G6-H6-I6-J6)*E8%`

or

`=(SUM(E5:J5)-SUM(E6:J6))*E8%`

but these are rather tedious, and clumsy. The easiest way to produce the result we require is to use an array formula.

`{=SUM(E5:J5-E6:J6)*E8%}`

Excel 5.0 for Windows uses curly brackets to denote array formulae.

When you've typed in the array formula (omitting the curly brackets; *Excel* inserts these for you), press [Ctrl]-SHIFT-RETURN. Removing the braces from the array formula does not produce the correct result:

`SUM(E5:J5—E6:J6)*E8%`

fails because the SUM function needs to be applied to both ranges separately. When you use an array formula, *Excel 5.0 for Windows* recognises this need, and implements it for you.

Using array formulae for interpolation

Look at the next illustration.

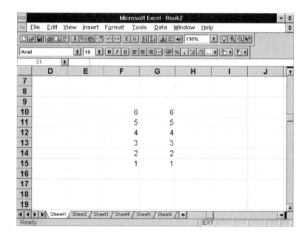

Here, simple values have been entered in F10:F15 and G10:G15. These values correspond to the demonstration given under 'Arrays' earlier.

We want to multiply F10 by G10, F11 by G11, F12 by G12, F13 by G13, F14 by G14 and F15 by G16. We could enter individual formulae in the range H10:H15.

    F10*G10 in H10
    F11*G11 in H11
    F12*G12 in H12

and so on. However, we can persuade *Excel 5.0 for Windows* to do this for us. Select H10:H15. Press [=]. Type in the following:

`=F10:F15*G10:G15`

Cell references

There's an easier way to enter cell references than typing them in. After you've pressed [=], use the mouse to select the necessary range. *Excel* surrounds it with a moving, dashed line and inserts the reference into the formula.

Now type *. Select G10:G15 in the same way. Press [Ctrl]-SHIFT-RETURN, irrespective of which technique you've used to select the ranges. The array formula is inserted, complete with curly brackets. This is the result.

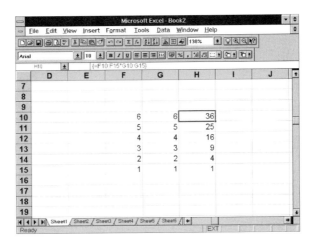

Each cell in the range H10:H15 contains the following array formula:

`{=F10:F15*G10:G15}`

Editing array formulae

Select the cell which contains the formula. *Excel 5.0 for Windows* displays the array formula in the Formula

Bar. Click in the Formula Bar; *Excel* removes the curly brackets. Make the necessary changes or additions. When you press [Ctrl]-SHIFT-RETURN to insert the revised formula, *Excel* re-inserts the brackets.

Editing

One difference between editing normal formulae and array formulae is that the individual cells within arrays can't have their contents changed. Nor can they be deleted or cleared.

Series

In Chapter 5, we looked at one aspect of a particularly useful *Excel 5.0 for Windows* feature: AutoFill (see 'Using AutoFill').

AutoFill is one technique for defining series. We'll use it – and others – in the next example.

A series is a succession of values arising from the first, either linearly or exponentially.

An example of series in action

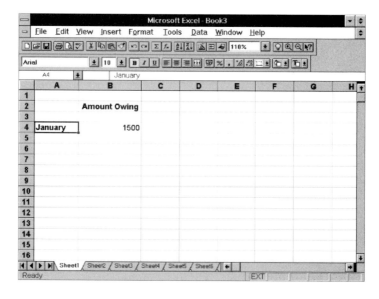

This rather simplistic worksheet will track the extent
to which the amount outstanding under a loan
decreases month by month. In January, £1,500 is
outstanding. We need to:

1.   Continue the month series in A4:A15

2.   Decrease the value in B4 by a fixed percentage (say,
5%) over the range B4:B15

Here's how to do these.

Applying a series to A4:A15

[January] has already been typed into A4. Select
A4:A15. Pull down the [Edit] menu and choose [Fill],
[Series]. In the [Type] section of the [Series] dialogue,
choose [AutoFill].

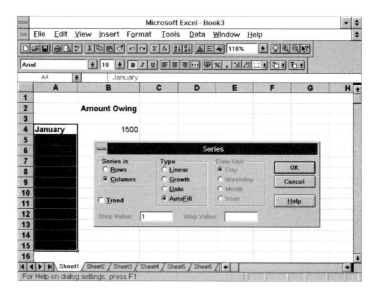

Examples of the series types you can use AutoFill to
complete are:

46, 49, 52, 55, 58 ...

18, 19, 20, 21, 22 ...

Monday, Tuesday, Wednesday, Thursday ...

12-May, 12-August, 12-November ...

AutoFill

AutoFill overrides the following [Series] dialogue features:

- Any entry in the [Step Value] box (see later)
- Any option in the [Date Unit] section (see later)

Applying a series to B4:B15

Select B4:B15. Pull down the [Edit] menu and choose [Fill], [Series]. In the [Type] section of the [Series] dialogue, click on [Growth]. In the [Step Value] field, enter [0.95].

We've just told *Excel 5.0 for Windows* to multiply the value in B4 by 95%. It then multiplies the resulting value in B5 by 95%. Again, C5 is multiplied by 95%. And so on. This is the result.

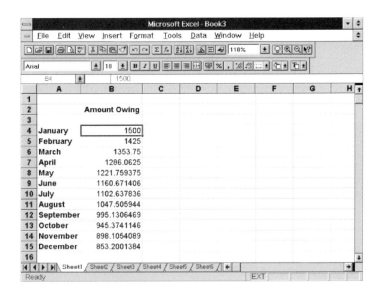

Rounding up

To round up the values in B4:B15 to two decimal places, do the following. Select B4:B15. Right-click in the selected range. Choose [Format Cells] in the short-cut menu. The [Format Cells] dialogue launches. Click on the [Number] tab if isn't already displaying. Highlight [Number] in the [Category] field. Highlight [0.00] in the [Format Codes] field. Choose [OK].

Other series

Linear series

On the previous page we see a [Growth] series. This
means that it multiplies successive cell values by the
figure in the [Step Value] field. *Excel* could use addition rather than multiplication. To do this, choose
[Linear] in the [Type] field. Look at the next illustration.

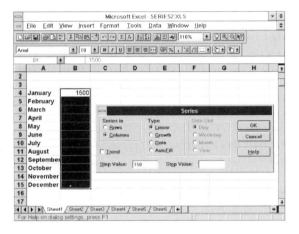

Here we have a similar situation. However, in this
instance we want to add 150 to each cell in B4:B15.
We've therefore invoked the [Edit] menu and chosen
[Fill], [Series]. In the [Type] section of the [Series]
dialogue, [Linear] has been selected. We've entered
[150] in the [Step Value] field. Choose [OK].

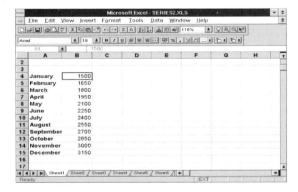

Date series

You can also create series based on dates. Here's how to do this. We'll work with the [Linear] series we created in the last example. Select A4:A15 and press [Delete]. Click in A4 and type in **1/1/94**. *Excel* converts this to **01/01/94**.

Select A4:A15. Pull down the [Edit] menu and choose [Fill], [Series]. In the [Type] section of the [Series] dialogue, click on [Date]. In the [Date Unit] field, click on the type of increment you require.

Choosing [Weekday] makes *Excel* promote each cell within the specified range to the next weekday. Selecting [Month] would promote each cell by one month.

If you chose [Month], and also entered a [Step Value] of [3], each cell would be advanced by three months.

 Use the [Stop Value] field to set the value at which the series should end.

If you want to change the date format *Excel* uses, do the following. Select the range. Right-click over the selection. Choose [Format Cells] from the short-cut menu which launches. In the [Format Cells] dialogue, click on the [Number] tab if it isn't already active. Choose [Date] in the [Category] list. Select the date format you want in the [Format Codes] list. Choose [OK].

Using the Fill handle

We discussed the use of the Fill handle to copy cell contents in Chapter 5 (see 'Using AutoFill'). You can also use the Fill handle to apply series. Look at the next illustration.

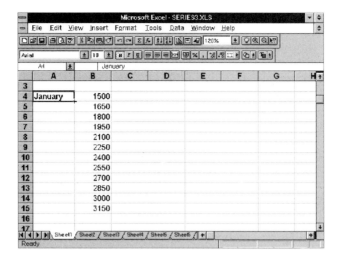

A4 has been selected, and the mouse pointer has been positioned over the Fill handle. If you drag the pointer (now in the form of a cross) down to A15 and release the mouse button, *Excel* increments the series.

Hold down Ctrl

If you hold down [Ctrl] when you move the mouse pointer over the Fill handle, it acquires a smaller cross to one side of the original. Dragging the Fill handle now produces one of the following effects, based on individual circumstances:

1. If *Excel* would normally increment the initial value, it doesn't.

2. If the initial cell contains a simple value which *Excel* would normally copy, it increments it.

This means that holding down [Ctrl] while you drag A4 to A15 simply copies [January] into each cell within the range.

Dragging the Fill handle up or to the left decreases a series.

Fill hanble

If you use the Fill handle to decrement a series, make sure you drag it beyond the first column or the top row. If you don't, *Excel* erases cell data within the specified range.

Trends

You can perform basic trend extrapolation from within the [Series] dialogue. Here's how to do this.

1. Type in two or more values in cells which are within the relevant range.

2. Select the whole of the range in which you want *Excel* to create the series.

3. Pull down the [Edit] menu and choose [Fill], [Series]. In the [Type] section of the [Series] dialogue, choose [Linear] or [Growth]. Click on [Trend] (*Excel* ignores any value in the [Step Value] field).

Trends

There's an easier way to do this.

Follow [1.] above. Select the range, then right-click on the Fill handle. Hold down the right mouse button and drag the handle over the range. When you release the button, a short-cut menu appears.

Choose [Linear] or [Growth]. Look at the next illustration.

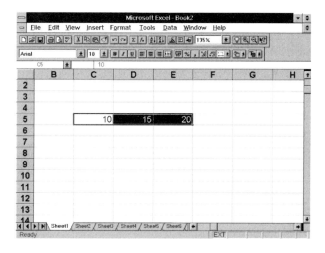

Here we have three values in successive cells. Using either of the Trend techniques we've just discussed produces the following:

Linear Trend   Growth Trend

The first illustration is a Linear extrapolation over successive rows, the second a Growth trend over successive cells in the one row.

 When it calculates the best equation to apply to Linear or Growth trends, *Excel* will amend the entries you entered originally, if necessary, to make them conform to the equation.

Links

Excel lets you create dynamic data links. You can link worksheet data in the same workbook and link separate workbooks.

The advantage of linking is that it's 'dynamic'. This means that, if two sets of data are linked, amending one automatically updates the second. *Excel* links data by inserting special formulae known as external references ('external', because they refer to cells in other worksheets). If two workbooks are linked, the workbook which contains the special formula is known as the 'dependent' workbook, while the other is the 'source' workbook.

Linked worksheets are frequently used to set up 'master' worksheets which focus and centralise totals from other worksheets.

Linking data in the same workbook

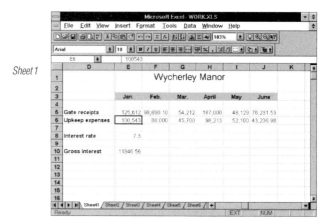

Sheet 1

We worked with the previous illustration in an earlier chapter.

Sheet 2
created in the same
workbook as Sheet 1

Here we've created a second sheet – Sheet 2 – in the same workbook. This sheet shows the breakdown for the expenses which formed row 6 in Sheet 1. B14 in Sheet 2 is the January expenses total and appears in E6 in Sheet 1.

Clearly, it would be useful to link E6 in Sheet 1 with B14 in Sheet 2, so that if we changed any of the (rather silly) amounts in column B in Sheet 2, the revised total in B14 would be reflected in Sheet 1. Here's how to do this.

1. Open the necessary workbook (see 'Opening Existing Workbooks' in Chapter 3 if you're unsure how to do this).

2. Click on the sheet tab at the base of the screen which represents the 'master' sheet – in this case, [Sheet 1].

3. Select the relevant cell (E6 here).

4. Press [=] to signal that you're about to enter a formula.

5. Click on the tab for the subsidiary sheet, in this case [Sheet 2].

6. Click in the relevant cell (B14 here) and press ENTER.

Excel inserts a special formula into E6 on Sheet 1:

`=Sheet2!B14`

Linking separate workbooks

Carry out the following steps to link separate workbooks. For the sake of example, we'll assume that the two worksheets which were the subject of 'Linking Data in the Same Workbook' above are now in separate workbooks WORK.XLS and BOOK3.XLS.

1. Open the two workbooks you want to link.

2. Pull down the [Window] menu and click on the master workbook entry at the base of the menu. In this case, [WORK.XLS].

3. Select the relevant sheet tab – Sheet 1, here – if it isn't already open.

4. Click in the cell (E6, here) which you want to host the linking formula.

5. Type [=].

6.   Now repeat steps 2 and 3, but this time select the second workbook (BOOK3.XLS) and the relevant sheet within it – Sheet 2 (2).

7.   Click in the cell (B14, here) which holds the data you want to link. Press ENTER.

Given the above, the formula inserted into E6 in Sheet 1 of WORK.XLS would be:

```
='[BOOK3.XLS]Sheet2 (2)'!$B$14
```

The single quotation marks are there because the worksheet name incorporates a space:

```
Sheet2 (2)
```

Workbook names are surrounded with square brackets. The sheet name is separated from the source location by an exclamation mark.

Updating worksheet links

If two worksheets within the same workbook are linked, or two worksheets within separate workbooks, *Excel 5.0 for Windows* handles the whole update process itself, behind the scenes.

However, there are a few complications with workbook-to-workbook links. If you open the dependent workbook (the workbook which contains the special formula) while the source workbook (i.e. the workbook which doesn't contain the special formula) isn't open, *Excel* asks if you wish to re-establish links. Click on [Yes] so that *Excel* updates the linked information to take account of any revisions. [No] makes *Excel* retain the earlier information when it opens the dependent workbook.

If only the source workbook is open and you change the relevant data, *Excel* will update the dependent workbook automatically when you open it.

Manual updating

You can update worksheet links manually, if you
want. Make sure the dependent worksheet is open.
Pull down the [Edit] menu and choose [Link]. The
[Links] dialogue launches.

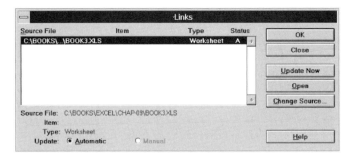

In the [Source File] box, highlight the link you want
to update manually. Click on [Update Now].

The [Update Now] button is greyed out – and
unavailable for use – if the data in the source and
dependent workbooks are identical.

If you want to change the link, click on [Change
Source]. The [Change Links] dialogue appears.

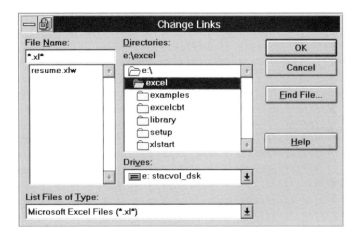

Use this to select a new source file (by locating the appropriate directory and file).

 Choose [Open] if you want to open the source workbook and update the link at the same time.

10

Styles and filter/sort operations

Now you can add some style! You'll work with *Excel's* built-in styles to save time and effort. You'll also set up your own, as well as 'What-if' tables and lists. Need to carry out sort operations? They're covered as well.

10

Styles and filter/sort operations

In this chapter we look at:

- Styles
- What-If tables
- Lists/Databases
- Sort operations

Styles

We've already looked at some styles (in Chapter 6, for instance, we examined currency, comma, percent and border styles briefly). In this chapter, we'll look at them in greater detail.

Styles are collections of associated formatting commands. The commands you can include are defined by the tabs in the [Format Cells] dialogue.

You can use the pre-defined styles which come with *Excel 5.0 for Windows*, and you can easily create your own. You can even copy styles from one workbook to another (normally, styles only apply to the workbook in which they were created).

The beauty is that you can apply a whole series of features with a few clicks of the mouse. Once styles are in force, if you want to change any aspect of the

associated formatting, you simply amend the style;
Excel then looks through your worksheet and amends
every instance of the style automatically, and quickly.

Applying styles

To impose a style on specific cells, select the
appropriate range. Pull down the [Format] menu and
choose [Style]. In the [Style] dialogue, click on the
arrow to the right of the [Style Name] field. From the
drop-down list, select the style you want to apply.

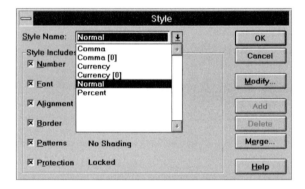

If there are aspects of a particular style which you
don't want to apply, deselect the appropriate category
in the [Style Includes] section. For instance, if you
don't want the selected cells to be protected, click on the
[Protection] check box to disable it.

Choose [OK] to implement.

Amending styles

When you alter a style which has been applied to
selected cells, *Excel* automatically updates all
instances of it throughout the current workbook.

Pull down the [Format] menu and choose [Style]. In
the [Style] dialogue, click on the arrow to the right of

the [Style Name] field. In the drop-down list, select the style you want to amend. Click on the [Modify] button. *Excel* launches the [Format Cells] dialogue.

Activate the tab which contains the formatting feature you want to amend. Make the necessary changes. Choose [OK] when you've finished to return to the [Style] dialogue. Click on [OK] here to amend all occurrences of the style.

Normal style

Of the pre-defined styles supplied with *Excel*, [Normal] is something of a special case. By default, every cell within every worksheet in every workbook has the [Normal] style applied to it. If you make any changes to [Normal], the amendments affect every cell within the current workbook.

Deleting styles

Invoke the [Style] dialogue, as above. In the [Style] dialogue, click on the arrow to the right of the [Style Name] field. In the drop-down list, select the style you want to delete. Click on the [Delete] button to proceed.

Creating your own style

There are two ways to create your own style. This is the first, and longest.

The formal way to create a style

Pull down the [Format] menu and choose [Style]. In the [Style] dialogue, click within the [Style Name] field. Enter a name for the new style. Click on [OK] to create the new style with the current [Format Cells] settings.

If you want to customise any of the settings first, however, click on the [Modify] button instead. *Excel* launches the [Format Cells] dialogue. Activate the tab which corresponds to the formatting category you want

to amend and make the necessary changes. Repeat
this process as often as necessary, then choose [OK] to
create the style based on your amendments.

The quick way to create a style

Select a range of cells to which you've already applied
the formatting features you want the new style to have.
Pull down the [Format] menu and choose [Style]. In
the [Style] dialogue, click inside the [Style Name] field.
Type in a new style name. Choose [OK]. *Excel* creates
the new style and automatically incorporates the
correct formatting features.

**Formatting
features**

If you use the method discussed in 'The Quick Way to
Create a Style', you should bear in mind that if you
select multiple cells with varying formatting features,
only those features which are common to all the cells
will be inserted in the style.

The style button

Excel 5.0 for Windows provides a very useful [Style]
button.

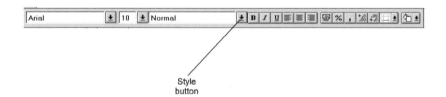

Style
button

However, *Excel* doesn't display this button until you
tell it to. For details of how to insert the [Style] button
in a toolbar, see Chapter 12. The [Style] button serves
as an excellent short-cut.

Using the button to impose styles

When you want to apply a style to selected cells, simply
click on the down-pointing arrow to the right of the

button. Click on the relevant style in the drop-down list. *Excel* applies the style immediately.

Using the button in style creation

Use the button in conjunction with the quick style creation method discussed in 'The Quick Way to Create a Style' above. Here's how to do this.

Select a range of cells to which you've already applied the formatting features you want the new style to have. Click on the arrow to the right of the [Style] button. Type in a name for the new style. Press ENTER to create the new style based on the specified formatting.

Copying styles to another workbook

This can be a useful device. If you've redefined a style in one workbook and want to save yourself the time and effort involved in recreating it in a second workbook, simply copy it across. Here's how to do this. Open both workbooks. Pull down the [Window] menu and click on the relevant workbook entry (choose the workbook to which you want to copy the styles).

You can't select which styles to copy: you have to copy all the resident styles.

Pull down the [Format] menu and choose [Style]. In the [Style] dialogue, choose [Merge]. The [Merge Styles] dialogue launches. In the [Merge Styles From] field, highlight the style whose styles you need to copy. Choose [OK]. Click on [Close] in the [Style] dialogue.

'What-if' tables

Excel lets you extrapolate predictions based on current figures and formulae. Look at the next example.

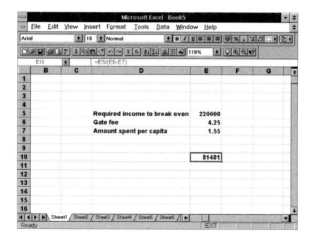

Wycherley Manor have made some rather simplistic
decisions which will, however, serve as a useful
example. They need a minimum income (from gate
receipts and other sources) of £220,000 to break even.
Research has shown that each visitor to the House
spends an average of £1.55 when they get inside. The
current gate fee is £4.50, and clearly inadequate.
Wycherley Manor need to know how many visitors
they have to attract, if they vary the gate fee, in order
still to produce the minimum income.

The number of visitors is given by the formula:

`=E5/(E6-E7)`

This has been inserted in E10. Based on the above
figures, *Excel* has calculated that 81,481 visitors are
required to break even.

Persuading *Excel 5.0 for Windows* to substitute revised
figures into the formula is easy. Let's say that
Wycherley have decided to try six new estimates for
gate fees. One of them is a reduction in the original
figure, the others are increases. These have been
entered in D11:D16.

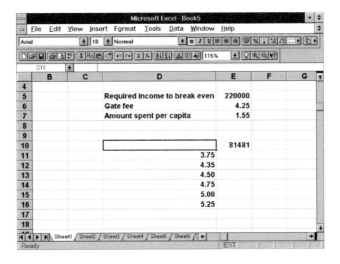

It's important to leave the cell to the left of E10 (the target formula) blank.

To produce the 'what-if' projection, do the following.

1. Select D10:E16

2. Pull down the [Data] menu and choose [Table].

3. In the [Table] dialogue, click in the [Column Input Cell] field. Enter a reference to the component of the formula which alters. In this case, we're inserting multiple values for the gate fee, so type in [E6].

4. Choose [OK].

Required income to break even	220000
Gate fee	4.25
Amount spent per capita	1.55
	81481
3.75	100000
4.35	78571
4.50	74576
4.75	68750
5.00	63768
5.25	59459

There are some further points to bear in mind.

The target formula – E10, here – must be positioned one row above and one column to the right of the values you enter, if you enter them in columnar format. If you enter values in rows, however, the target formula must be placed one row below and one column to the left.

If you enter rows, rather than columns, of values, you should complete the [Table] dialogue – see step [3.] – differently. Enter the reference to the component of the formula which alters in the [Row Input Cell] field instead of the [Column Input Cell] box.

'What-if' projections with two variables

Let's take the Wycherley Manor example a step further. So far, we've entered one variable – differing gate fees – into the formula and calculated the revised number of visitors. But what if Wycherley want to insert two variables?

It so happens that Wycherley have been investigating various schemes for increasing the amount people spend inside the House. Obviously, if this figure increases they'll need fewer visitors to break even.

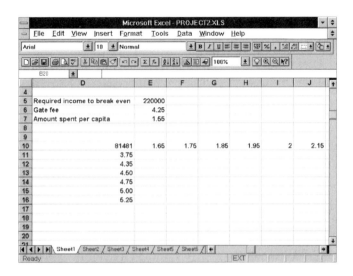

We've made several changes to the original table. The range D11:D16 is unaltered. However, the formula in E10 has been moved to D10: two-variable projections require that the formula should be situated in the upper left corner of the relevant range. In addition, a row of variables has been inserted.

We can now calculate the number of visitors required when both variables alter. For instance, *Excel* will enter in E11 the number of visitors if:

the gate fee is £3.75 AND
the amount spent per capita is £1.65

Here's how to do this.

1. Select the relevant cell range (in this case, D10:J16).

Make sure you include the formula as well as the row and column variables.

2. Pull down the [Data] menu and choose [Table]. In the [Table] dialogue, click in the [Row Input Cell] field. Insert a reference to the formula component which relates to row variables: in this case, E7. Click in the [Column Input Cell] field. Insert a reference to the formula component which relates to column variables: in this case, E6.

Click on [OK] to generate the what-if table.

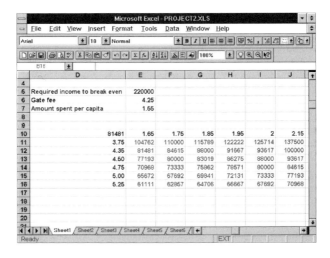

Microsoft Excel - PROJECT2.XLS

	D	E	F	G	H	I	J
4							
5	Required income to break even	220000					
6	Gate fee	4.25					
7	Amount spent per capita	1.55					
8							
9							
10		81481	1.65	1.75	1.85	1.95	2	2.15
11		3.75	104762	110000	115789	122222	125714	137500
12		4.35	81481	84615	88000	91667	93617	100000
13		4.50	77193	80000	83019	86275	88000	93617
14		4.75	70968	73333	75862	78571	80000	84615
15		5.00	65672	67692	69841	72131	73333	77193
16		5.25	61111	62857	64706	66667	67692	70968
17							
18							
19							
20							

Arrays

When it creates a what-if projection, *Excel* inserts an array formula (for information on the use of arrays, see 'Arrays' in Chapter 9). This means that if you need to you can change any of the variables in either a one-variable or a two-variable projection; *Excel* will recalculate the table.

Here's an example. In the completed two-variable what-if table, the [Amount spent per capita] variable in F10 has been altered from 1.75 to 1.80. As a result, the range F11:F16 has been recalculated automatically:

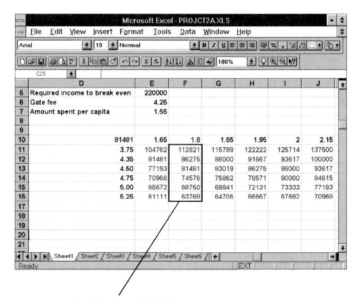

Excel has recalculated
this range automatically

Lists

Excel 5.0 for Windows has comprehensive database capabilities.

Excel also calls databases 'lists'.

In *Excel*, databases store information within a worksheet; they have a rectangular structure. The rows are known as records, and the columns fields. The row at the top of the database holds the field names.

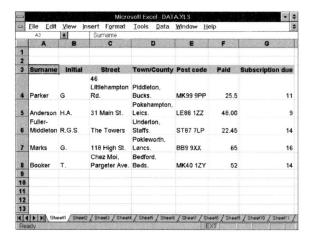

This is a fairly simple *Excel* database, listing subscribers to a magazine. There are seven field names:

- Surname
- Initial
- Street
- Town/County
- Post Code
- Paid
- Subscription due

The following are requirements for *Excel* databases:

1. The field names must be entered in the row at the top of the database range.

2. Each field name must be unique.

3. Use each row in the database for one record only.

4. Don't leave blank rows between records.

5. Ensure that each field (column) represents only one data type.

It's also a good idea (though not essential) to:

1. Apply a distinctive formatting of some kind to the field names.

2. Surround the database with at least one blank column and row.

3. Create only one database per worksheet.

These measures help to make the database more visually effective.

Field entries can contain:

* Number values
* Text
* Dates/times
* Formulae

Field names, on the other hand, can only hold text (up to 255 characters).

 It's usually best to create only one database per worksheet.

Excel imposes no limits on the size of the databases you create, other than the normal worksheet restriction (i.e. 256 columns x 16,384 rows).

Now let's look at operations you can perform on databases.

Data Form

The Data Form is a very useful aid to database management. You can use it to:

* Edit existing database records
* Browse through records
* Restore earlier versions of records
* Delete records
* Add new records
* Conduct searches through the database

You don't need to use Data Form to do this. You can perform all of these operations directly on the database itself, if you want, using standard *Excel5.0 for Windows* row and column manipulation techniques. However, Data Form makes the whole process much more convenient. Here's how to use Data Form.

Click on the relevant sheet tab to activate the worksheet which contains the database. Select any cell within the database, or select the entire database. Pull down the [Data] menu and choose [Form].

Excel creates a dialogue based on your database.

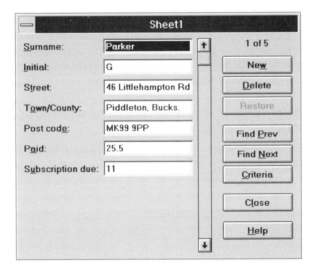

Your field names appear on the left of the dialogue. On their right are text entry boxes which list field entries. Data Form automatically displays the first record. From here, you can perform various actions.

Editing records

Simply click in the appropriate text box and amend the contents. Choose [Close] when you've finished.

Moving through the database

To view other records, you can either:

1. Use the vertical scroll bar to travel through the database until you find the record you want, or

2. Click on [Find Prev] or [Find Next] to view the previous or next record, respectively.

Restoring records

Click on [Restore] to reinstate the original, unaltered version of the current record.

Restoring records

When you move to a different record, using either of the methods described in 'Moving Through the Database', *Excel 5.0 for Windows* saves any amendments you've made to the current record. This means that you can only restore records if you haven't yet moved to another record or closed Data Form.

Deleting records

Move to the record you want to delete. Click on the [Delete] button. *Excel 5.0 for Windows* warns you that the deletion will be permanent.

Choose [OK] to erase the record from the database, or [Cancel] to return to the Data Form without proceeding with the deletion.

You can't use *Excel's* Undo feature while Data Form is active.

Adding new records

Click on [New] in the Data Form. *Excel* produces a special version of Data Form with blank fields. Complete these as necessary. When you've finished defining the new record, press ENTER. *Excel* saves the new record and the Data Form displays with blank fields again. If you want to create another new record, repeat the above procedure. If not, choose [Close] to close Data Form.

Searching through the database

Click on the [Criteria] button. *Excel* displays a special version of Data Form (it has [Criteria] in the top right hand corner).

The boxes which represent each field in the database are blank. Click in the box which corresponds to the field you want to search through and type in the relevant search criterion. Then click on the [Find Next] button to locate the first record which meets your criteria. Choose [Find Next] as often as necessary (or click on [Find Prev] to backtrack through flagged records).

Here's an example. If you want to search for all records whose subscriptions are renewable on issue 14, enter [14] in the [Subscription due] field.

Wild cards

You can use standard wild cards to widen the scope of searches. [*] represents one or more non-specific characters. [?] stands for one unspecified character.

For example, to find all records whose towns or counties begin with [B], enter [B*] in the [Town/county] field. *Excel* finds the two records whose names are: Booker and Harter. To flag the record in the name of Parker, you'd have to enter [?B] or [*B] into the [Town/county] field.

You can also use *Excel's* comparison operators to narrow search criteria. These operators are:

=   equal to

<   less than

>   greater than

<=   less than or equal to

>=   greater than or equal to

<>   not equal to

For example, to locate records where subscriptions are due with issue 12, or later, you'd enter >=12 in the [Subscription due] field.

Criteria

If you complete more than one field in the [Criteria] version of Data Form, you should bear in mind that *Excel 5.0 for Windows* will only find records which fulfil ALL of the criteria. In other words, *Excel* processes multiple criteria as AND conditions in Boolean logic.

When you've finished searching for criteria, clicking on [Close] shuts down Data Form and returns you to your database.

Setting up criteria ranges

Excel 5.0 for Windows provides an extension of the [Criteria] feature. You can set up criteria ranges and then filter them. When you do this, *Excel* 'hides' all records which don't match the selection criteria.

Let's say we want to flag all records in which:

[A]

1.   The surname begins with P, and

2.   The post code doesn't begin with MK, and

3.   The [Paid] field shows more than 25

We also want a second set of criteria, flagging records where:

[B]

1.   The surname begins with any letter in the range: A to L, and

2.   The post code begins with MK, and

3.   The [Paid] field shows more than 35

We want to find records which match either [A] or [B]. For this, we need a criteria range.

Here's how to set up a criteria range. Select a row
above your database.

Don't select a row below your database, or to one side:
if you do, later operations may obscure the criteria
range.

Type in a row of field names. You can use any of the
field names which are already present in your database, but you don't have to use them all.

In the row below, type in the criteria you want *Excel* to
search for. To fulfil [A] above, enter (in successive cells
within the row):

P*   **<>MK***   **>25**

To meet [B], enter (again in successive cells, but this
time – because we're operating an [A] OR [B] search –
in the row below):

<M   **MK***   **>35**

This is our final criteria range:

	A	B	C
1	Surname	Post code	Paid
2	P*	<>MK*	>25
3	<M	MK*	>35

Filtering the criteria range

Filtering displays database records which match
the specified criteria while hiding those which don't.
Here's how to apply a criteria range as a filter.

First, define a criteria range (see 'Setting up Criteria
Ranges' on the previous page). Then select any cell
within the database. Pull down the [Data] menu and
choose [Filter], [Advanced Filter].

The [Advanced Filter] dialogue launches. *Excel 5.0 for Windows* inserts the reference for the database range in the [List Range] field. Click in the [Criteria Range] field. If *Excel* hasn't already entered it, type in the reference for the criteria range (or use the mouse to define the range).

Make sure the [Filter the List, in place] option is selected in the [Action] section. Click on [OK] to filter the database in line with the specified criteria range.

This is the result.

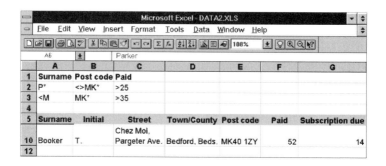

Copying filtered records

If you select [Copy to Another Location] in the [Action] section of the [Advanced Filter] dialogue, instead of [Filter the List, in-place], you can copy the filtered records to another location within the current worksheet. To do so,

1. Make sure *Excel* has entered the reference for the database range in the [List Range] box.

2. Click in the [Criteria Range] field. If *Excel* hasn't already entered it, type in the reference for the criteria range (or use the mouse to define the range).

3. Click in the [Copy To] field and enter the reference of the cell which you want to form the upper left corner of the new range.

4. Choose [OK].

You can, if you want, copy the filtered records to a second worksheet. To do this, activate the sheet to which you want to copy the records. Pull down the [Data] menu and choose [Filter], [Advanced Filter]. Select [Copy to Another Location]. Click in the [List Range] field, then click on the sheet tab for the worksheet which holds the database and criteria range. *Excel* switches to this sheet. Use the mouse in the normal way to define the database range.

Click in the [Criteria Range] field; *Excel* returns you to the second worksheet. Click once more on the sheet tab for the worksheet which holds the database and criteria range; *Excel* returns to this. Use the mouse to define the criteria range. Click in the [Copy To] field. *Excel* switches to the second worksheet again. Use the mouse to select the cell you want to form the upper left corner of the new range. Click on [OK] when you've finished.

The illustration on the next page shows our filtered range being transferred to Sheet 2 in the same workbook. The mouse has been used to define A3 as the upper left corner of the new range.

Copying filtered records

To copy filtered records to a sheet in another workbook, open the destination workbook first. Follow steps [1.] and [2.]. Click in the [Copy To] field. Pull down the [Window] menu and click on the entry at the base of the menu which relates to the second workbook. *Excel* switches to the other workbook. Activate the relevant sheet by clicking on its tab and enter the reference of the cell which you want to form the upper left corner of the new range in the [Copy To] field. Click on [OK].

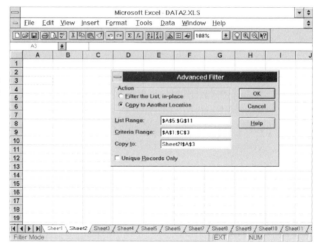

The filtered range in the process of being transferred to Sheet 2 in the same workbook.

Removing the filter

To go back to viewing all records within the database, pull down the [Data] menu and choose [Filter], [Show All].

Using AutoFilter

AutoFilter is a feature which is new to *Excel 5.0 for Windows*.

In essence, it's a simpler form of the type of filter operation we performed in 'Filtering the Criteria Range' above. However, AutoFilter is an extremely useful technique in its own right. Here's how to use AutoFilter.

Activate the worksheet which contains your database. Select any cell within the database. Pull down the [Data] menu and choose [Filter], [AutoFilter].

Excel goes through your database and inserts drop-down arrows on the field names. To apply a filter, click on the arrow to the right of the relevant field and select the appropriate option. For instance, to view only those records whose surnames are Parker, click on the arrow to the right of the [Surname] field name. Select [Parker] from the drop-down list. This is the result.

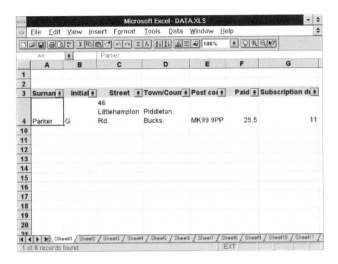

Notice that the arrow to the right of the [Surname] field name is now blue, to indicate that a filter is in operation in the associated field. Repeat the above with any of the other field names, if necessary.

  You can only apply one AutoFilter at a time

You can only choose one item from any AutoFilter drop-down list. For instance, if you select [Parker] in the [Surname] list, and then invoke the list again and choose [Harter], only the record for [Harter] will display. If you need multiple selections, see 'Customising AutoFilter' in the next section.

Special options

Each AutoFilter drop-down list has four special options:

All

Displays all records in the field.

Custom

Produces a special dialogue you can use to apply multiple criteria (see 'Customising AutoFilter' below).

Blanks

Displays only those records which have blank cells in the current column.

NonBlanks

Displays only those records which have non-blank cells in the current column.

Customising AutoFilter

Click on the down-pointing arrow to the right of any AutoFilter field name. Choose [Custom] from the list. The [Custom AutoFilter] dialogue launches. This has four fields which you can use to define one or two selection criteria.

 If you require more than two selection criteria, you need to apply *Excel's* Filter feature to a criteria range. See 'Setting up Criteria Ranges' and 'Filtering the Criteria Range' above.

Setting up the first criterion

Click on the upper down-pointing arrow on the left of the dialogue. This produces a list of comparison operators (see 'Searching Through the Database' earlier for information on these).

Select the appropriate operator. Click on the arrow to the right of the criterion box. This launches a list of unique entries in the current field. Select the one you want.

Selecting the second criterion

This is optional. If you need to, repeat the procedures discussed in 'Setting up the First Criterion' but this time in respect of the second row.

If you do this, you must also select either [And] or [Or]. [And] insists that records must fulfil both criteria, while [Or] specifies that a hit with either criteria is sufficient.

When you've finished with the [Custom AutoFilter] dialogue, choose [OK] to apply the criteria you've specified. Records which don't match them are hidden.

Disabling AutoFilter

To view the database in its entirety again, pull down the [Data] menu and choose [Filter], [AutoFilter]. *Excel* unchecks the [AutoFilter] option, and all the records are displayed.

Sort operations

You can sort databases into alphabetical, numerical or date order, or into a sequence of your own choosing. You can also sort columns of worksheet data.

Excel's sort operations are based on the allocation of three 'keys'. Keys are the user-specified fields around which *Excel* bases its sort operations, and are arranged hierarchically. For instance, if you wanted the magazine subscribers' database we created earlier sorted in surname order, the [Surname] field would be the main key. If you wanted subscribers with the same surname arranged in the order of their initials, the [Initial] field would be the second key. If, additionally, you wanted subscribers with the same name and initial ordered in terms of subscriptions paid, the [Paid] field would be the third key.

You can order database records in Ascending or
Descending order. This applies equally to
alphabetical, numerical and date sorts.

Sorting databases

Select any cell in the database. Pull down the [Data]
menu and choose [Sort]. *Excel* selects the whole of the
database automatically, and the [Sort] dialogue
launches.

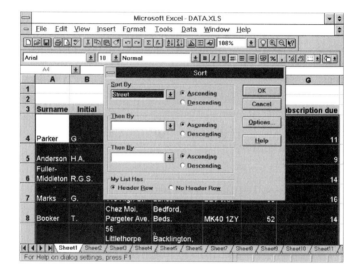

To select the first key, click on the down-pointing arrow
to the right of the [Sort By] field. In the list which
appears, select the field you want to be the first key.

If you need a second key, repeat this procedure for the
first [Then By] field. If you need a third key, do the
same with the second [Then By] field.

The header row

If *Excel* detects that a database has a header consisting
of field names, the [Header Row] option in the [My List

Has] section should be selected automatically. This means that the header isn't included in the sort. If there is no header, *Excel* should detect this and select [No Header Row].

Before you begin a sorting operation, make sure that the correct option has been activated.

The [Options] button

If you need it, you can carry out a case-sensitive sort.

For instance, if there were two records in our subscriber index, one with the name [Parker] and the other [parker], *Excel* would place [Parker] first.

You can also use the [Options] button to sort columnar data (see 'Sorting Columnar Data' over the page).

Choose [OK] to initiate the sort.

 For simple sorts (based only on one key), do the following. Select one cell in the column you want to use to sort your database. Then click on the [Sort Ascending] or [Sort Descending] buttons in the [Standard] toolbar.

Sort Descending
button

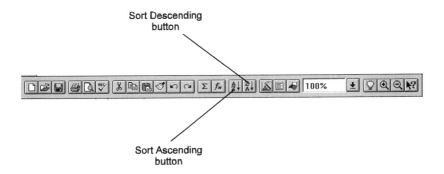

Sort Ascending
button

Sorting columnar data

Follow the procedures discussed in 'Sorting Databases'
above. However, there's one additional step. When
you've launched the [Sort] dialogue, click on the
[Options] button. In the [Sort Options] dialogue, select
[Sort Left to Right] in the [Orientation] section. Click
on [OK] to return to the [Sort] dialogue. Allocate the
necessary keys and choose [OK] to sort the data.

Graphics and charts

Need more pizzazz? You can liven up your worksheets with clip-art, and you can apply a variety of formatting effects to inserted pictures. You can also insert, format and print charts of all types.

11

Graphics and charts

In this chapter, we look at:

- Working with graphics images
- Working with charts
- Printing charts

Graphics images

Excel 5.0 for Windows will happily incorporate clip art in a variety of third party formats into your worksheets.

 Adding commercial clip art to worksheets is a useful technique for increasing their impact.

Inserting images into your worksheets

Activate the relevant worksheet first. Pull down the [Insert] menu and choose [Picture]. The [Picture] dialogue appears.

Use the [Directories] box to select the directory in which the graphics image you want to use is situated. Highlight the file in the list under the [File Name] field.

 If you want to see what the image looks like before you use it, click on [Preview Picture]. *Excel 5.0 for Windows* displays a thumbnail of the picture in the [Preview] box.

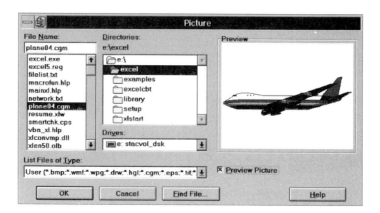

Click on [OK] to import the image.

The next illustration shows an amended version of
SALES.XLS, a sample worksheet supplied as standard
with *Excel 5.0 for Windows*.

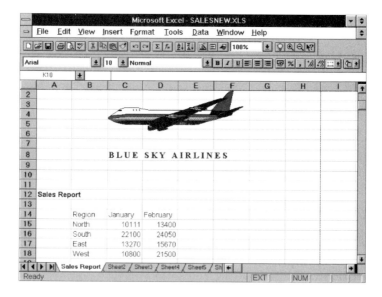

A clip art image has been added. This image is in CGM
(Computer Graphics Metafile) format, just one of the
many formats *Excel* will convert. The image has had

some formatting options performed on it (see 'Formatting Pictures' over the page).

Amending inserted pictures

Most images, when you've imported them into *Excel
5.0 for Windows*, will require some work before they're
quite right. You may have to reposition or resize them.
You can also apply a variety of formatting options.

Resizing images

Excel automatically surrounds imported pictures with
a border. The image fill also obscures the worksheet
cell structure ('Formatting Pictures' in the next section
provides more detail on how to remove image borders
and make cells display through the empty sections of
pictures). Additionally, they're usually too big.

To resize the image, click on it once with the left mouse
button. *Excel* surrounds it with a black frame (in this
case, indistinguishable from the border) and drag
handles.

Click and hold on one of the handles. Drag it inward to
shrink the image or outward to expand it.

If you hold down a SHIFT key while you drag any one of
the corner handles, *Excel 5.0 for Windows* will resize
the image proportionately, maintaining the original
height/width ratio.

Release the mouse button to confirm the operation.

Moving images

Click within the image you want to move to select it.
Hold down the left mouse button and drag the image to
its new location. Release the button to confirm the
move.

Formatting pictures

Double-click on an inserted picture. This produces the
[Format Object] dialogue. Select the [Patterns] tab.

The Patterns tab

Use this to control border, shadow and fill options.

By default, *Excel 5.0 for Windows* surrounds each
imported graphic with a border. To turn this off, choose
[None] in the [Border] section. If you want the border
to remain but wish to customise it, choose [Custom]. To
alter the border style, click on the arrow to the right of
[Style] and select the appropriate style from the list. To
alter the border colour, click on the arrow to the right of
[Color]; select the appropriate colour from the list. To
amend the border thickness, click on the arrow to the
right of [Weight] and select the appropriate weighted
line from the list.

Excel also imposes a fill around all imported graphics.
It surrounds the graphic itself with a rectangle filled
with white. The result is that the underlying cell grid is
hidden. If you don't want this, choose [None] in the
[Fill] section. If you want to customise the automatic
fill, click on the appropriate colour in the coloured
square.

If you want to impose a pattern, click on the arrow to
the right of the [Pattern] field. Select a pattern from
the graphic list which appears. If you want to select a
colour as well as a pattern, repeat this procedure but
select a colour from the graphic list. To impose a
shadow effect on a picture, click on [Shadow]. When
you've finished, choose [OK].

Other ways to insert pictures

Using the clipboard

You can use the *Windows* clipboard as a way of
transferring an image from another program into
Excel 5.0 for Windows. For instance, if you have
CorelDRAW! on your system you can open an image in it
and work on it. When you've finished, you can then
copy this to the clipboard. Switch to *Excel* and activate
the appropriate worksheet. Pull down the [Edit] menu
and choose [Paste]; the image is inserted into your
worksheet.

OLE links

With other programs which support OLE, you can
insert graphics into *Excel* and have them dynamically
linked to the original images.

 OLE – or Object Linking and Embedding – is a set of
standards developed by Microsoft. They allow for
reciprocity between images (called 'objects').

In other words, if you have two copies of an image, one
within the originating program and one in *Excel*, if an
OLE link has been established you can amend the
original and have the copy in *Excel* updated
accordingly, without any action on your part. To go
back to our *CorelDRAW!* example, you can work on an
image in *CorelDRAW!*. As you experiment with design
variations, you can see the results in situ in *Excel*.

Moreover, double-clicking on the linked graphic within
Excel launches the originating program.

You can also insert *Excel* charts and worksheets as
linked objects within other programs. For instance,
you could insert a chart as an object within a *Word 6.0*

for Windows document; with an OLE link in force, any amendments you make to the chart in *Excel* itself will be reflected automatically in *Word's* version.

To insert a linked image into *Excel 5.0 for Windows*, open the relevant worksheet first. Pull down the [Insert] menu and choose [Object]. The [Object] dialogue launches.

Select the [Create New] tab if it isn't already active. In the [Object Type] field, highlight the type of object you want to insert. Choose [OK]. *Excel* inserts a picture holder into your worksheet and the originating program launches.

Create the object (in this case, a graphic) you want to work with. As you do so, a linked copy appears in *Excel*. As you work on the image, the copy is updated (you can see this by regularly switching between the source program and *Excel*).

Charts

Excel 5.0 for Windows lets you create charts based on worksheet information. Charts summarise data visually and make it much easier to absorb. There are two basic types of chart:

- Charts created on the same sheet as the relevant data
- Charts created on separate sheets

To help you create charts, *Excel* provides ChartWizard. ChartWizard leads you by the hand through the entire process of chart creation.

Creating charts on the same sheet

Look at the illustration opposite.

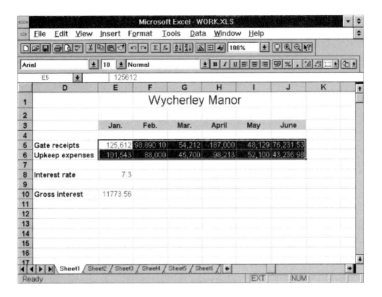

This is a sample worksheet we created in an earlier chapter. Cells E5:J6 have been selected. Let's use ChartWizard to create a chart based on the data they contain.

The first step in the chart creation process is to select the range you want to chart; we've already done this. Pull down the [Insert] menu and choose [Chart], [On This Sheet].

Alternatively, click on the ChartWizard button in the [Standard] toolbar.

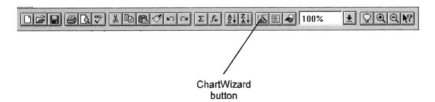

ChartWizard
button

Excel surrounds the selected range with a moving, dashed line. Additionally, the mouse pointer changes to a cross complete with a small chart icon. Click with this anywhere within the current worksheet to establish the initial chart size (you can resize it later if you want to). Alternatively, click and hold with the left mouse button and drag with the pointer to define the chart area now.

**Defining
chart area**

If you hold down one SHIFT key as you define the chart area, *Excel* inserts a perfect square rather than a rectangle. If you hold down the [Alt] key while you drag, *Excel* aligns the chart with the underlying cell grid. Hold down both keys to do both.

Release the mouse button to confirm the operation. The first ChartWizard dialogue launches. Check in the [Range] field to make sure that *Excel* has entered the appropriate cell range. If it hasn't, type in corrected details. Click on [Finish] to create the chart immediately, using the default format.

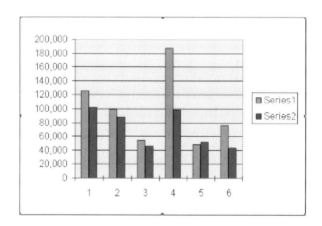

If you want to apply your own format, click on [Next] instead of [Finish] and complete the remaining ChartWizard dialogues.

**[Back]
button**

To backtrack to an earlier dialogue at any stage in the use of ChartWizard, click on the [Back] button. To abort ChartWizard at any time, without creating a chart, choose [Cancel].

In the next ChartWizard dialogue, click on the new chart type.

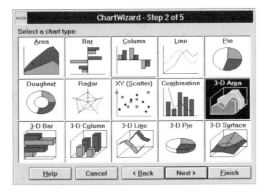

Choose [Next]. The ChartWizard Step 3 dialogue launches. Select the chart sub-format you want to use. Click on [Next]. The Step 4 dialogue launches. Use this to specify how *Excel* should base its chart on the worksheet data.

 The options available in this dialogue vary according to which chart format you've chosen.

Note that the [Sample Chart] field reflects changes you make to the chart.

To determine the orientation, click in the [Data Series In] section. By default, *Excel* chooses [Rows]. To formulate the chart on columns, click on [Columns].

In our present example, if [Rows] is selected, the first data series in the chart reflects E5:J5 in the original worksheet. If you choose [Columns], however, the first series is based on E5:E6.

If you want the first row or column of the data to be used as labels or text rather than as a data series, do the following. In the [Use First ... Row(s)] field, specify the rows you want *Excel* to use as labels/text. In the

[Use First ... Column(s)], specify the columns you want *Excel* to use as labels/text. Choose [Next] when you've finished.

Step 5 is the final ChartWizard dialogue. Choose [Yes] in the [Add A Legend] section to insert a legend. If you need to insert a title, click in the [Chart Title] field and type in the text you want *Excel* to use. Click in the [Category], [Axis] or [Series] fields if you want to title these, then type in the relevant text. Choose [Finish] when you're ready; ChartWizard creates the chart based on your specifications.

Creating a separate chart sheet

You can create a new sheet automatically and place the chart on this. Or you can place the chart on an existing sheet within the current workbook.

Creating a new sheet

Select the data range. Pull down the [Insert] menu and choose [Chart], [As New Sheet]. Step 1 of ChartWizard launches. Follow the instructions in 'Creating Charts on the Same Sheet'. When you've finished with ChartWizard, choose [Finish]. *Excel* creates a new worksheet entitled Chart1 and places this to the left of the current worksheet.

Selecting an existing sheet

Select the data range. Position the mouse pointer over the sheet tab for the worksheet you want *Excel* to place the chart on. Right-click and select [Insert] from the short-cut menu which appears. The [Insert] dialogue launches.

Highlight [Chart] in the [New] field and choose [OK]. The Step 1 dialogue of ChartWizard launches. Follow the instructions in 'Creating Charts on the Same

Sheet'. When you've finished with ChartWizard, choose [Finish]. *Excel* creates a new chart in the worksheet you specified.

Using ChartWizard to amend an existing chart

You can use ChartWizard to amend existing charts, but only to a limited extent (see 'Formatting and Editing Charts' later for further information on revising existing charts).

Here's how to do this. Click on the chart to select it. Then click on the ChartWizard button in the overhead [Standard] toolbar. When used in this way, ChartWizard provides only two of its five standard dialogues. These correspond to the Step 1 and Step 4 dialogues discussed earlier in 'Creating Charts on the Same Sheet'.

Use the first, if necessary, to amend the cell range on which the chart is based. Use the second to alter the data series orientation. Click on [OK] when you've finished.

Formatting and editing charts

You can edit existing charts in a variety of ways. You can also apply various formatting enhancements.

To reformat or edit a chart embedded within a worksheet, double-click in it; *Excel* surrounds it with a coloured, thicker border.

 If the chart is too large to fit on-screen, *Excel* launches a special temporary chart window.

The [Insert] and [Format] menus now contain chart-specific commands. Note that, if you're working with a chart sheet rather than an embedded chart, these commands are automatically available without your having to select the chart.

Inserting new chart components

You can insert titles, legends, data labels, axes, gridlines and even pictures.

Inserting a title

Pull down the [Insert] menu and choose [Titles]. The [Titles] dialogue launches. The fields for any titles already present in the chart are checked. To insert another title, click an unchecked box and choose [OK]. *Excel* inserts a new placeholder into the chart. To define it, click in the Formula Bar and type in the title. Press ENTER to insert the completed title.

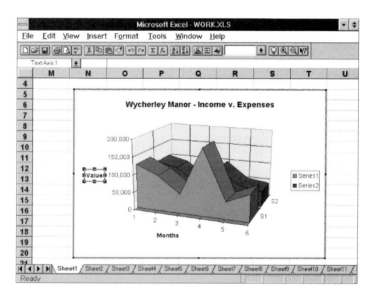

Inserting data labels

Pull down the [Insert] menu and choose [Data Labels]. In the [Data Labels] dialogue, click on the labels you want to appear on the chart. Choose [OK].

Inserting legends

To insert a legend, pull down the [Insert] menu and choose [Legend].

If a chart already has a legend (as the example we're working with here does), choosing [Legend] will have no effect.

Inserting axes

You can control whether axes are visible. Pull down the [Insert] menu and choose [Axes]. In the [Axes] dialogue, deselect any of the axes you don't want to display.

3D chart formats have three axes, other formats only two.

Choose [OK].

Inserting gridlines

You can specify the size of gridlines which *Excel* applies to charts. Pull down the [Insert] menu and choose [Gridlines]. In the [Gridlines] dialogue, select [Major Gridlines] and/or [Minor Gridlines] in any of the available axes.

Inserting pictures

Pull down the [Insert] menu and choose [Picture]. In the [Picture] dialogue, highlight the graphic file you want to insert into your chart. For how to do this, see 'Inserting Images into your Worksheets' earlier. Choose [OK] to proceed.

Inserting additional data series

Pull down the [Insert] menu and choose [New Data]. In the [Range] field in the [New Data] dialogue, type in the reference for the range you want to add. Choose [OK]; *Excel* incorporates the new series in the chart.

Formatting charts

Before we examine major options on the [Format] menu in some detail, some further information about chart structure.

Excel charts consist of individual components which you can isolate. Components include:

- The plot area
- The legend
- Axes
- Axis titles
- Data series
- Gridlines
- The chart title

For instance, if you want to reformat the Chart Title specifically, click on it to select it. *Excel* surrounds it with a frame, complete with drag handles. You can now move or resize it using standard mouse techniques.

To reformat the title, double-click on its frame. Or pull down the [Format] menu and choose [Selected Chart Title]. This produces the [Format Chart Title] dialogue.

 The dialogue format depends on the chart component selected.

The tabs in the [Format Chart Title] dialogue are very similar to the equivalent tabs in the [Format Cells] dialogue. For how to use this dialogue, see Chapter 4.

Other components

Double-click on any chart component to produce the specific formatting dialogue. Select the tab you need (if appropriate). Choose the relevant options and click on [OK] to confirm.

The [Format] menu

Use this to:

1. Reformat selected chart components

2. Apply a different chart type to existing charts

We've already dealt with [1.]; see above.

To amend chart types, double-click within the current chart (or activate a chart sheet). Then pull down the [Format] menu and choose [Chart Type]. In the [Chart Type] dialogue, choose either [2-D] or [3-D] in the [Chart Dimension] section.

Click on the icon which corresponds to the new chart type you want to use. Choose [OK] to amend the chart accordingly.

If you want to choose a new chart sub-type, click on [Options] in the [Chart Type] dialogue after you've selected the new chart type.

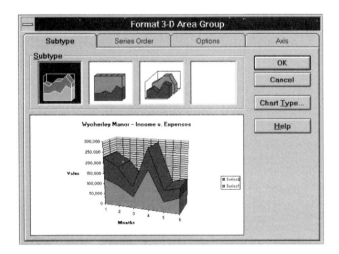

Select the [Subtype] tab if it isn't already active. In the [Subtype] section, choose the new sub-type. Click on [OK] to amend the chart accordingly.

Using the chart toolbar

Excel has a special [Chart] toolbar which you can also use to choose a new chart type.

To activate the [Chart] toolbar, pull down the [View] menu and choose [Toolbars]. In the [Toolbars] section of the [Toolbars] dialogue, click on [Chart] to select it. Click on [OK]. The [Chart] toolbar launches. Click on the arrow to the right of the [Chart Type] button.

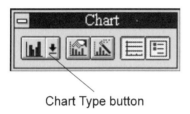

Chart Type button

Select the new chart type from the drop-down graphical list.

Using AutoFormat

Use the [AutoFormat] option in the [Format] menu as a convenient way to change an existing chart's layout.

Select the chart or chart sheet. Choose [AutoFormat] in the [Format] menu. Select a chart type in the [Galleries] box. Choose a sub-format in the [Formats] section. Click on [OK] when you've finished.

Printing charts

You can't print charts embedded in worksheets in isolation: you can only print them along with the worksheet data. (See 'Printing' in Chapter 8 for how to do this). However, you can print chart sheets separately. Here's how to do this. Activate the chart sheet by clicking on the relevant sheet tab.

To print the chart sheet, pull down the [File] menu and choose [Print]. In the [Print] dialogue, click on the [Page Setup] button. In the [Page Setup] dialogue, activate the [Chart] tab if it isn't already selected.

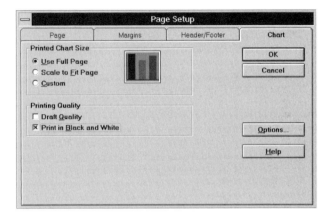

 You can also initiate printing by clicking on the [Print] button in the [Standard] toolbar.

Print button

This prints the chart immediately – without launching the [Print] dialogue – based on the current settings. In the [Printed Chart Size] section, select the relevant option:

[Use Full Page]

Stretches the chart disproportionately and makes it fill the page.

[Scale to Fit Page]

The chart fills as much of the page as possible without distortion.

[Custom]

Prints the chart at the size shown on screen.

Choose [Print in Black and White] if you're printing a colour chart to a black and white printer. If you don't do this, *Excel 5.0 for Windows* will convert colours to grey-scales, and it may be difficult or impossible to differentiate between the various data series.

Choose [OK] when you've finished. Back in the [Print] dialogue, click in the [Copies] text entry box if you want to print more than one copy of the chart sheet and enter the number of copies required. Choose [OK] to begin printing.

12

Customising *Excel*

Now you'll give *Excel* the look you want by customising screen components and setting overall *Excel* preferences. Need some tips? Run Tip Wizard. Use Info Window for precise details of cell formatting, and Find and Replace to substitute data quickly and easily.

12

Customising *Excel*

In this chapter, we look at the following:

- How to customise toolbars
- TipWizard
- General preferences
- Info Window
- Find and Replace operations

Toolbars

Toolbar buttons provide very useful short-cuts to *Excel* operations. *Excel* comes with 13 pre-defined toolbars, each with a variety of buttons representing the commonest operations. Only two toolbars display as standard, although you can arrange for as many as you want to appear (see 'Toolbars' in Chapter 3 for more information on how to do this). Additionally, you can determine where toolbars appear on the screen and what shape they are. You can easily add your own buttons from a reserve pool. You can even create your own toolbars.

Customising screen position and shape

Some of *Excel's* toolbars, when invoked, anchor themselves at the top of the screen (e.g. the [Standard] and [Formatting] toolbars which display by default). Others – for instance, the [Chart] toolbar which we

looked at in 'Using the Chart Toolbar' in Chapter 11 –
are more outwardly mobile, and even have their own
title bar.

This division is deceptive, however. All *Excel 5.0 for
Windows* toolbars can be re-shaped and repositioned
on the screen at will.

Moving a toolbar

Click anywhere within the toolbar area, but make sure
you don't click on a button. Hold down the mouse
button and drag the toolbar to the new location.
Release the button to confirm the move. The next
illustration shows a blank *Excel* screen when the
[Standard] toolbar has been moved.

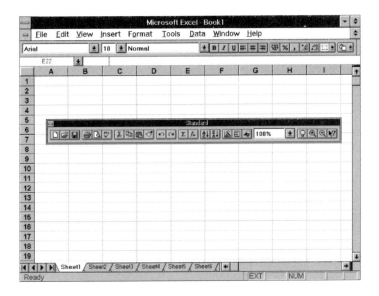

**Special
screen
areas**

Excel designates four screen areas as special. If you
move toolbars to the top, bottom, right or left screen
edges, they 'anchor' themselves. This doesn't mean
they can't be moved. However, toolbars in these areas
provide a firm base from which to launch their
associated features.

Resizing toolbars

To reshape a toolbar, move the mouse pointer over any border; it turns into a double arrow. Drag the toolbar into a new shape. The next illustration shows sizing variants on the [Chart] toolbar.

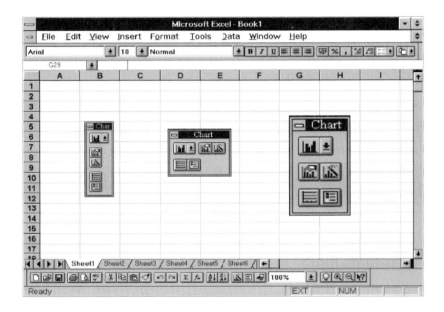

Not all toolbars will berth adequately on the left or right page edge. Some, like [Chart], simply sit there without anchoring themselves. This is because they contain buttons which produce drop-down lists. Others, however, such as the [Microsoft] toolbar – which allows you to launch other Microsoft programs at the click of a button – do attach themselves satisfactorily. Combine toolbar reshaping with repositioning until you achieve the 'look' you want.

Adding buttons to existing toolbars

The first step is to display the toolbar to which you want to add new buttons. To do this, right-click on an existing toolbar. Select the toolbar you want to amend from the drop-down list.

If no toolbars are currently visible, you have to use a different method. Pull down the [View] menu and choose [Toolbars]. In the [Toolbars] field in the [Toolbars] dialogue, click on the entry for the toolbar you need to activate.

 You can also use the [Toolbars] dialogue to make some generalised statements about toolbar buttons.

Deselect [Color Toolbars] to display buttons without colour. Choose [Large Buttons] to allocate more space to buttons, and less to worksheets. Deselect [Tool Tips] if you don't want to display the yellow help text when you move the mouse pointer over buttons.

Choose [OK] when you're ready. Now right-click on the toolbar you want to add buttons to. *Excel* launches a short cut menu. Click on [Customize]. Its dialogue appears.

Excel divides toolbar buttons into categories. Highlight the correct category in the [Categories] field; associated buttons are displayed to the right.

 To find out a button's function, move the mouse pointer over it and click with the left mouse button. *Excel* displays some brief explanatory text in the bottom left-hand corner of the dialogue.

To add one of the buttons to the relevant toolbar, click and hold on the button. Drag it out of the [Toolbars] dialogue and onto the toolbar.

Choose [Close] when you've finished.

 You can add the same button to as many toolbars as you want.

In the following illustration, the [Style] button has been dragged onto the [Standard] toolbar.

The Style button has been
dragged to the toolbar

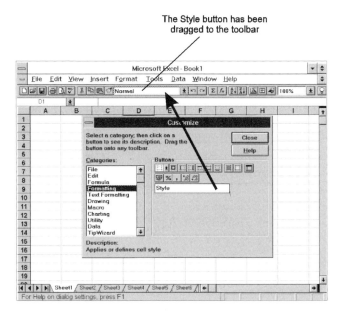

Removing buttons from toolbars

Taking buttons off toolbars is even easier. Display the
relevant toolbar. Left-click and hold on the button you
want to remove. Drag the button off the toolbar into
the worksheet area. Release the mouse button to
complete the operation.

You can apply the button to any other toolbar by using
the methods discussed in 'Adding Your Own Buttons to
Existing Toolbars' above. Removing buttons has no
effect on their entry in the [Customize] dialogue.

Creating your own toolbars

Right-click on any existing toolbar, then choose
[Toolbars] from the resulting short-cut menu.
Alternatively, if no toolbar is currently displaying pull
down the [View] menu and choose [Toolbars]. In the
[Toolbars] dialogue, click in the [Toolbar Name] field.

Type in a name for your new toolbar (replacing any
name currently displayed). As you start typing, *Excel*

5.0 for Windows makes the [New] button available.
When you've entered the new name, click on [New].
Excel creates a new toolbar. It also opens the
[Customize] dialogue.

Add as many buttons to the new toolbar as you need.
For how to do this, see 'Adding Your Own Buttons to
Existing Toolbars' above. As you add buttons to the
new toolbar, *Excel* adjusts the size and shape
accordingly.

Create a new toolbar

There's a quicker way to create a new toolbar. From
within the [Customize] dialogue, drag a button you want
to include in a new toolbar into the worksheet area.
Excel 5.0 for Windows creates a new toolbar
automatically and includes the button. *Excel* also
allocates a name to the new toolbar ('Toolbar 1', or
similar).

When you've finished adding buttons to the new
toolbar, choose [Close]. The [Customize] dialogue
closes, leaving the new toolbar open.

TipWizard

This is a specialised toolbar. Its function is to monitor
what you do and offer timely and appropriate tips.
When TipWizard detects that you've just done
something on which it can provide advice, the bulb in
the TipWizard button in the [Standard] toolbar 'lights
up' (it turns yellow). Click on the [TipWizard] button to
see what it is.

You can also display TipWizard more or less
permanently by selecting [TipWizard] in the
[Toolbars] section of the [Toolbar] dialogue – see

earlier. In the next illustration, *Excel* is displaying the [TipWizard] toolbar.

TipWizard button

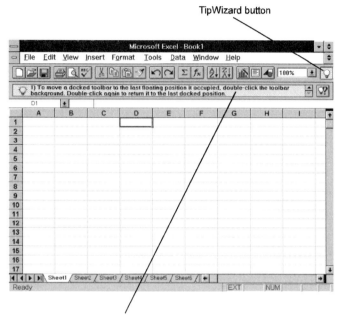

TipWizard toolbar

TipWizard retains a record of all tips which have been offered during the current session; use the up and down arrows to the right of the TipWizard toolbar to scroll through them.

Extra button

Sometimes, when you've just initiated an action which TipWizard determines could have been carried out more easily or quickly, a special button appears to the right of the toolbar. The extra button is 'live': you can click on it to see how the feature it represents works.

Often, TipWizard displays a special [Help] button.

Click on this for more information on TipWizard's suggestion.

The Tip of the Day

TipWizard also offers random suggestions under the
guise of a Tip of the Day. To view this, use the scroll
bars to the right of TipWizard to move to the first tip.

Excel 5.0 for Windows displays a Tip of the Day each
time you start it (as long as the [TipWizard] toolbar
was displaying when you last closed *Excel*).

General Preferences

Excel 5.0 for Windows gives you a lot of control over the
way it works. In this section, we'll look at those areas
which concern screen appearance and overall
operation.

Pull down the [Tools] menu and choose [Options]. The
[Options] dialogue launches. Like many *Excel*
dialogues, the [Options] dialogue is organised into
tabs.

The [View] tab

If it isn't already activated, click on the [View] tab for
precise control over the *Excel* screen.

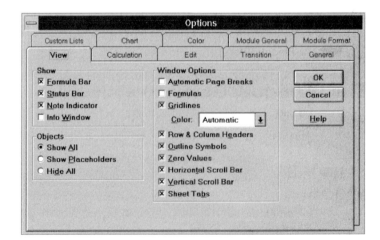

The [Show] section

Check any options you need here to ensure that they display. Note that the [Show] section settings aren't stored with the current workbook when you save it (settings in the other sections are). Here are some brief notes:

Note indicator

If you don't want *Excel* to display a small red dot in the upper-right corner of cells which have hidden notes (see 'Cell Notes' in Chapter 7), deselect this option.

Info window

Check this to display the Info window for the current worksheet (see the section covering 'Info Window' on page 234).

The [Objects] section

Check [Show All] to display all graphics objects. Check [Show Placeholders] to display selected pictures and charts as grey rectangles. Objects which aren't selected display normally.

Select [Show Placeholders] when you need to speed up *Excel's* scrolling.

Check [Hide All] to hide all graphics objects. Note, however, that when objects are hidden, they don't print.

Pressing [Ctrl]-[6] toggles between [Show All], [Show Placeholders] and [Hide All].

The [Window Options] section

Check any options you need here to ensure that they display.

Some brief notes:

Automatic page breaks

Check this option to display *Excel*-imposed page breaks.

Formulas

Check this option to display formulas in cells rather than the resultant values.

 Press [Ctrl]-['] to display formulas in cells rather than the resultant values.

Gridlines

Check this to display cell gridlines. Uncheck it to hide them.

Gridline Color

Click on the arrow to the right of the [Color] field to specify gridline colour. Choose the colour you want from the drop-down graphic list.

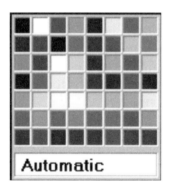

Row & column headers

Check this to display row and column headings.

Zero values

Uncheck this to display cells which contain zero values as blank cells.

Horizontal & vertical scroll bars

Check these to display the horizontal and vertical scroll bars.

Sheet tabs

Check this to display sheet tabs.

The General tab

Click on the [General] tab if it isn't already active.

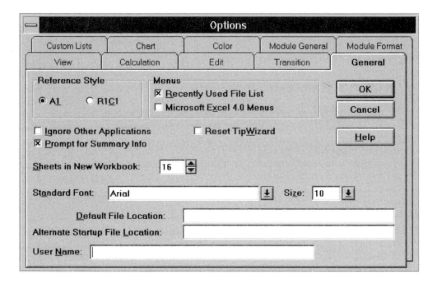

Here are some notes on especially useful features.

The reference style section

Check the [R1C1] option to label both columns and rows numerically.

Prompt for summary info

Check this to display the [Summary Info] dialogue when you save a new workbook. Complete any of the sections in the [Summary Info] dialogue. Click on [OK] to save your information with the host document.

Sheets in new workbook

To amend the default number of worksheets in any new workbook you create, click in the [Sheets in New Workbook] field. Type in the new number.

Standard font & size

To use a different typeface to display row, column and cell text, click on the arrow to the right of the [Standard

Font] field. Select the new font from the list which appears. To amend the type size, click in the [Size] field and type in the new point size.

 You have to close and restart *Excel* for the revised typeface and type size details to take effect.

Default file location

If the *Excel* files you're currently working with are contained in one directory, enter its full details here. This means that you don't have to specify the directory each time you open or save a workbook.

For instance, if you're working with files in a directory entitled C:\RETAIL\ACCOUNT, and you enter this in the [Default File Location] field, *Excel* will log on to this directory automatically when you invoke the [Open] or [Save As] dialogues.

Info Window

Excel provides a special window which lets you verify the contents of any active cell. Use the [Info] window to obtain a detailed – and fully customisable – statement of a cell's status.

In the current worksheet, select the cell you want the [Info] window to report on. To open the [Info] window, pull down the [Tools] menu and choose [Options]. If the [View] tab isn't active, click on it. In the [Show] section, choose [Info Window]. Click on [OK].

Excel 5.0 for Windows provides customised menus for the Info window. To specify which areas you want the [Info] window to report on, pull down the [Info] menu. Click on one of the options; the [Info] window display is updated. To include more than one extra option, repeat this process.

Tiling the Info Window

It's a good idea to keep the Info window alongside open worksheets, for ease of reference. To do this, pull down the [Window] menu in the [Info] window; choose [Arrange]. In the [Arrange *Windows*] dialogue, choose [Tiled]. Click on [OK]. *Excel* tiles the Info windows next to the current worksheet.

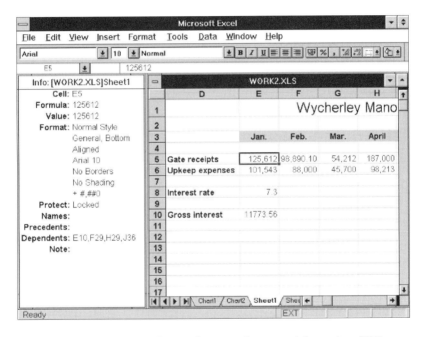

To close the Info window, make sure it's active (if it isn't, click on its title bar). Then press [Ctrl]-[F4].

Printing the Info Window

With the Info window active, pull down the [File] menu and choose [Print]. The [Print] dialogue launches. For how to complete this (and for information on the option buttons within the [Print] dialogue), see 'Printing' in Chapter 8.

Choose [OK] to print the Info window.

Using Find and Replace

In any worksheet, finding specific data easily is important. In large worksheets, it becomes imperative. Luckily, *Excel 5.0 for Windows* provides comprehensive data location capabilities. Once you've found the data you're looking for, you can also substitute new data in its stead.

Find operations

To conduct a search through an entire worksheet, position the cursor in cell A1.

 If you want to limit the search to specific cell ranges instead of the entire worksheet, select the range first.

Pull down the [Edit] menu and choose [Find]. Alternatively, press [Ctrl]-[F]. The [Find] dialogue launches.

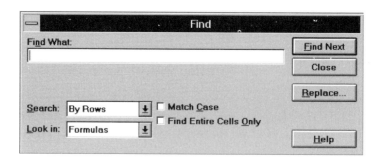

Type in the data you need to locate in the [Find What] box. To specify whether you want the search restricted to rows or columns, click on the arrow to the right of the [Search] field and make the appropriate choice from the drop-down list. To specify the worksheet component you want *Excel* to search through, click on the arrow to the right of the [Look In] field and make the appropriate choice from the drop-down list:

[Formulas]
Makes *Excel* look through cells which contain formulae

[Values]
Makes *Excel* look through cells which don't host formulae

[Notes]
Makes *Excel* look through cells which contain notes

 If you want *Excel* to find only those data entries whose case matches what you've typed in the [Find What] box, check [Match Case].

For instance, if you ask *Excel* to locate [TOTAL] and select [Match Case], *Excel* will ignore [Total] and [total].

Check [Find Entire Cells Only] to ignore cells where what you've typed in the [Find What] box forms part of a larger cell entry. For example, if you select [Find Entire Cells Only] and tell *Excel* to find `Total`, it will ignore a cell which contains `Year End Total`. It will only find cells which contain `Total`.

Click on [Find Next] to initiate the search. To find subsequent matches, click on [Find Next] again as often as necessary.

When you've finished with the [Find] dialogue, click on [Close] or press [Esc].

Find and Replace operations

Pull down the [Edit] menu and choose [Replace]. Alternatively:

1.   Press [Ctrl]-[H], or

2.   Follow the procedures discussed in 'Find Operations' to produce the [Find] dialogue, then click on the [Replace] button.

The [Replace] dialogue appears. Enter data you want *Excel* to locate in the [Find What] field. Type in the data you want substituted for it in the [Replace with] box. For information on how to complete the other fields in the [Replace] dialogue, see 'Find Operations' earlier.

When you've set the necessary search parameters, click on [Find Next] to locate the first match. Then:

1.   Click on [Replace] to carry out the substitution, or

2.   Click on [Find Next] to look for the next match without making the substitution.

You can replace all occurrences of the specified data automatically by clicking on [Replace All] at any time.

Choose [Close] when you've finished with the [Replace] dialogue.

13

Reports and summaries

Want to convert worksheet data
into reports and print the results?
Easy. You'll use the Pivot Table
Wizard temporarily to re-formulate
worksheet data. Need to import
data in non-*Excel* formats? Use
Text Wizard. Use Find File to locate
Excel files.

13

Reports/Summaries

This chapter covers:

- Reports (including View Manager and Scenario Manager)
- Scenario Summaries
- Some further *Excel* Wizards: Pivot Table; Text Wizard
- Find File

Reports

Excel 5.0 for Windows lets you print out reports.

In *Excel*, a report is the crystallisation of alternative ways of looking at worksheet data.

Reporting is usually the final stage in a three-tier process. You'll normally use *Excel's* Report feature after you've made use of two additional options, either singly or in unison:

- View Manager
- Scenario Manager

View Manager

View Manager lets you create and save to disk varying worksheet views with their host worksheet, without having to save them as separate worksheets.

Views are saved with host worksheet.

A view consists of a wide range of settings. For instance, you can save:

- window settings
- print settings
- sheet settings

Once a view has been defined and stored, you can invoke it – and edit it – at will. You can also print it as a report (incorporating different scenarios, too, if you need this).

Creating a view

Open the workbook you want to work with. Activate the sheet for which you want to create alternative views. Institute the worksheet settings you want to save as a view. This can involve:

- Invoking the [Page Setup] dialogue to establish print settings – see Chapter 8
- Resizing the current worksheet window – see Chapter 2
- Splitting or tiling the screen – see Chapter 2
- Setting the appropriate zoom level – see Chapter 2
- Making adjustments to *Excel's* preferences in the [Option] dialogue – see Chapter 12.

When you've finished, pull down the [View] menu and choose [View Manager]. The [View Manager] launches.

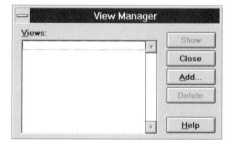

Previously defined views (if any) are listed in the [Views] section. To create a new view, click on [Add].

In the [Name] field in the [Add View] dialogue, type in a name for the new view.

It's a good idea to incorporate a reference to sheet titles in view names. This is because View Manager shows all views for the current workbook.

If you want the view to contain print settings, check [Print Settings]. If you want to incorporate details of hidden columns and rows, select [Hidden Rows & Columns]. Both of these options are automatically activated.

Choose [OK]. *Excel 5.0 for Windows* saves the view under the name you specified.

Displaying views

Open the relevant workbook. Pull down the [View] menu and choose [View Manager]. In the [Views] field within the [View Manager] dialogue, highlight the view you want to inspect and click on [Show]. *Excel* launches the worksheet view.

Delete view

To delete a view, highlight it in the [Views] field and click on [Delete]. *Excel* requests your confirmation before proceeding. Choose [OK] to go ahead with the deletion, or [Cancel] to back out.

Scenario Manager

Scenarios can be used as a useful 'what-if' tool. You can establish sets of values as scenarios and invoke them *en masse*.

For instance, you can set up a scenario which lists revised input values in a worksheet. You can then apply them to the worksheet with just a few mouse clicks, without affecting the worksheet data itself. This saves you the time and trouble of manually inserting the revised values, and removing them afterwards. You can also produce a report based on the 'what-if' scenario.

Scenarios

Scenarios work best with worksheets which are organised into definite input and output sections (values are entered and manipulated in some way, and the results displayed).

Here's how to create a scenario.

Defining a scenario

Open the appropriate worksheet. Pull down the [Tools] menu and choose [Scenarios]. The [Scenario Manager] launches.

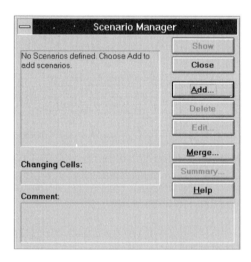

If this is the first time you've run Scenario Manager in the current worksheet, the [Scenarios] field will be greyed out. To create a new scenario, click on the [Add] button. The [Add Scenario] field launches.

Type in a name for the new scenario in the [Scenario Name] field. Next, click in the [Changing Cells] field. Outside the dialogue, use the mouse to point to the cells whose input values you want to re-enter in the new scenario (or enter their cell reference directly).

**Defining
your first
scenario**

It's a good idea to define your first scenario in the current worksheet using the present, rather than revised values. To do this, carry out the procedures which follow. Give your scenario a distinctive name: e.g. 'Base Values'. When you reach the [Scenario Values] dialogue, accept the values which *Excel* inserts.

By creating a scenario for your original worksheet values, you can return to it after you've explored 'what-if' situations.

In the next illustration, we'll define a scenario containing revised inputs for the range E5:J5. To be more precise, we'll increase the values in this range by 10% to see what happens to the Gross Interest value in E10.

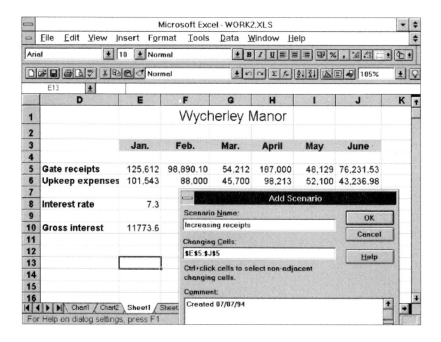

Click in the [Changing Cells] field. Note that *Excel* has surrounded E5:J5 with a moving dashed line to indicate that we've selected it for inclusion in the new scenario, and it's also entered the appropriate reference in the [Changing Cells] field.

If you want to, enter some brief descriptive text in the [Comment] field. This will help you identify the scenario later. *Excel* enters some text itself.

Click on [OK] when you've finished with the [Add Scenario] dialogue. *Excel* launches the [Scenario Values] dialogue.

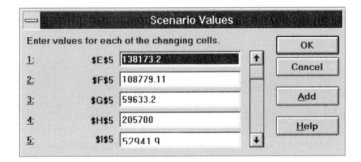

Enter the revised values.

 If there are more values than the [Scenario Values] dialogue can display (as there are here), use the scroll bars to move to them and enter the revised values

Choose [OK]. *Excel 5.0 for Windows* returns you to the [Scenario Manager] dialogue.

The new scenario is listed in the [Scenarios] field.
Create as many scenarios as you need.

Inspecting scenarios

To apply a scenario, highlight it in the [Scenarios] field
and click on the [Show] button in the [Scenario
Manager] dialogue.

The next two illustrations show the result of applying
the [Increasing Receipts] scenario we've just defined.
First, the [Base Values] scenario, without the value
amendments.

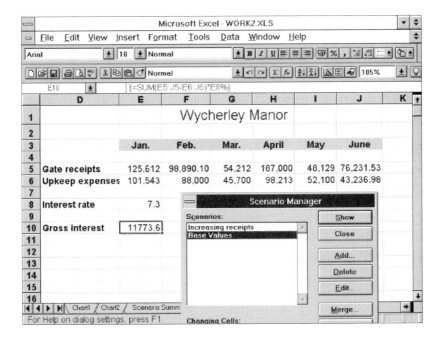

Now the [Increasing Receipts] scenario.

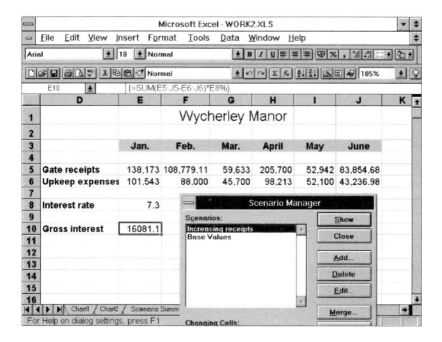

Notice that the range E5:J5 has been updated by the
[Increasing Receipts] scenario. E10 (which subtracts
the sum of E6:J6 from the sum of E5:J5 and multiplies
the result by 8%) has also been updated.

To return to pre-increase values, highlight [Base
Values] in the [Scenarios] field and choose [Show].

Scenario summaries

Before we go on to print a report based on View
Manager and Scenario Manager, let's take a brief look
at Scenario Summaries.

You can produce a special Scenario Summary sheet
incorporating all current scenarios. Here's how to do
this.

Open the worksheet for which you've created
scenarios. Pull down the [Tools] menu and choose
[Scenarios]. Click on [Summary]. The [Scenario

Summary] dialogue appears. Select [Scenario Summary] in the [Report Type] section, then click in the [Result Cells] field. Enter the reference for the cell or cells which carry the result of each scenario; in our present example, this is E10. Alternatively, point to the cell(s) with the mouse. Click on [OK] to create the Scenario Summary sheet.

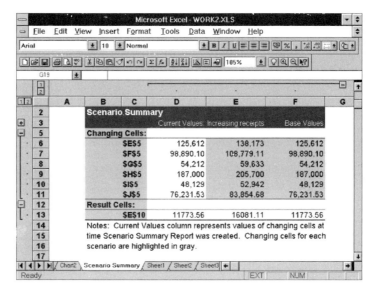

The cell values in grey are those which form the basis of the scenarios.

To return to your worksheet after you've finished with the Scenario Summary Sheet, click on the relevant tab.

Printing out a report

Open the workbook which contains the data you want *Excel* to report on.

To use *Excel's* report printing option to best effect, you should have followed the procedures in 'Creating a view' and 'Defining a scenario' earlier.

Pull down the [File] menu and choose [Print Report]. The [Print Report] dialogue launches. If you've invoked [Print Report] for the first time, the [Reports] section is greyed out.

Choose [Add] to create a new report. In the [Add Report] dialogue, click in [Report Name] and type in a name for the new report. Now do the following:

1. Click on the arrow to the right of the [Sheet] field. In the list which appears, select the sheet you want to base the report on.

2. Optionally, click on the arrows to the right of the [View] and [Scenario] fields; select the predefined view and/or scenario you want to apply to the report.

3. Click on [Add]. *Excel* summarises the instructions you've just given it in the [Sections in this Report] box.

Repeat the above steps as often as necessary, until you've included as many sections as you need in your report. Choose [OK].

Excel returns you to the [Print Report] dialogue. The report you've just set up is now listed in the [Reports] section. To print it, highlight it and click on [Print]. In the special [Print] dialogue which launches, enter the number of copies you need in the [Copies] field and click on [OK] to begin printing.

More Wizards

So far, we've looked at various *Excel* Wizards:

• ChartWizard, in 'Charts' in Chapter 11.
• TipWizard, in 'TipWizard', Chapter 12
• Function Wizard, in 'Entering Functions Using Function Wizard' in Chapter 9.

Now we'll examine two more: Pivot Table and TextWizard (for a discussion of TextWizard, see 'TextWizard' later on page 262).

Pivot Table

Pivot Tables are analysis tools to manipulate data in *Excel* databases. Look at the next illustration.

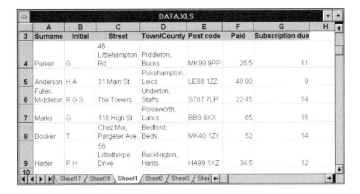

This is the database we created in Chapter 10; it lists the subscribers to a magazine, together with some subscription details. The data is currently organised fairly loosely into the following categories:

- Surname
- Initial
- Street
- Town/county
- Post code
- Paid
- Subscription due

If you want to reorganise this data in a different way, one way would be physically to amend the database. This can be a very time-consuming exercise. For instance, to restructure the data so that the [Surname] data is linked to [Subscription due] data, while at the same time totalling the amounts in the [Paid] field, would require a major overhaul, even the creation of a new database.

Fortunately, however, you can use Pivot Table to achieve this effect much more conveniently.

Setting up a Pivot Table

Open the worksheet in which you've set up the *Excel* database. Pull down the [Data] menu and choose [Pivot Table]. The first step of the Pivot Table Wizard launches.

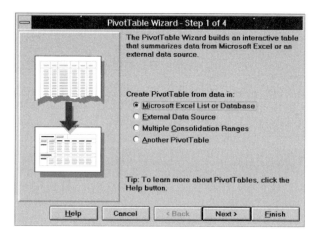

Make sure [Microsoft Excel List or Database] is selected.

You can create Pivot Tables from data outside *Excel* worksheets. However, this chapter will concentrate on doing so from worksheet databases.

Click on [Next]. Step 2 of the Pivot Table Wizard appears.

Excel inserts a cell reference in the [Range] field. If this isn't the correct range for your database, enter the correct reference. Click on [Next]. Step 3 launches.

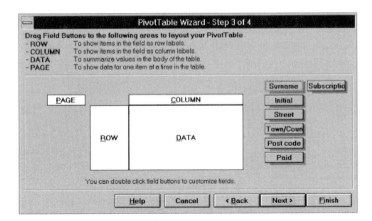

Use this to rearrange the database fields in the order
you want. Each field (a column header in the original
database) now appears as a button on the right of the
screen. Use the mouse to drag the relevant buttons to
the correct place in the main section of the dialogue.
There are four areas:

Column
Field items are arranged in columns with labels across
the top

Row
Field items are arranged in rows with labels across the
top

Data
Summarises pivot table values

Page
Displays one field item at a time

To return to our original example, we want to link the
[Surname] fields to [Subscription due] fields. We also
want to total the [Paid] field items and interrelate
these. Here's how to do this.

Drag the [Subscription due] button to the [Column]
area, [Surname] to the [Row] area and [Paid] to the
[Data] area.

You can customise the fields if you want. To do this, double-click on a field button. The [PivotTable Field] dialogue this produces is identical for any field.

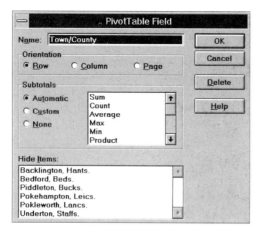

You can alter the field name; click in the [Name] field and type in the new title. To alter the orientation, select either [Row], [Column] or [Page] in the [Orientation] section. If you don't want *Excel* to calculate sub-totals where appropriate, select [None] in the [Subtotals] section. If you want to hide individual field items, select the items in the [Hide Items] section (you can make multiple selections by clicking on the relevant items). When you've finished, choose [OK]. Click on [Next].

In the fourth – and final – step in Pivot Wizard, click in the [PivotTable Starting Cell] box. Enter the reference for the cell at which you want the pivot table to be inserted in your worksheet.

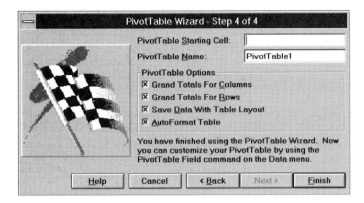

 If you leave the [PivotTable Starting Cell] box blank, *Excel* will create a new worksheet for the pivot table, next to the database sheet.

Excel automatically names the new pivot table. If you want *Excel* to use a different name, enter this in the [PivotTable Name] field. Click on [Finish] to create your pivot table. This is the result here.

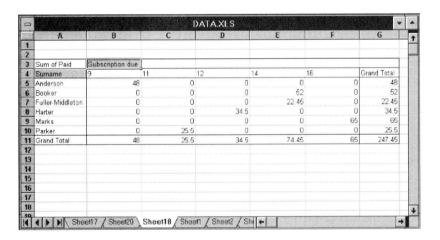

The Pivot Table Wizard has organised the [Surname] field items in consecutive rows. The columns contain the [Subscription due] items; there are only five because two subscribers – Booker and Fuller-Middleton – have their subscriptions due with issue 14. The [Paid] items are inserted into the table at the appropriate locations, and totalled horizontally and vertically.

The beauty of a pivot table is the ease with which you can manipulate the data.

You can't amend any of the values themselves within a pivot table; you can only change field and item names. When you do so, however, the changes aren't reflected in the original database.

You can do so visually, for the simple reason that the grey cells within a pivot table are buttons. You can move them to new locations by the simple expedient of clicking on them and dragging.

Here is one example of the kind of manipulation you can use a pivot table to perform. Look at the next illustration.

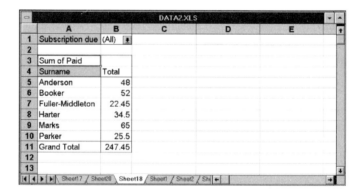

The [Subscription due] field has been dragged to a point outside the table. As such, its classification is automatically changed from [Column] to [Page].

We could have changed its classification by double-clicking on the button and selecting [Page] from the appropriate [PivotTable Field] dialogue.

Excel 5.0 for Windows also provides a short-cut menu
route to the [PivotTable Field] dialogue. Right-click
within a button. In the short-cut menu which
launches, choose [PivotTable Field]. The pivot table no
longer displays each item for the [Subscription due]
field. Instead, you have access to a drop-down list.
Click on the arrow to produce a list of field items.

Click on an item so the pivot table restricts the values it
displays accordingly. In the next illustration, [14] has
been selected in the [Subscription due] list.

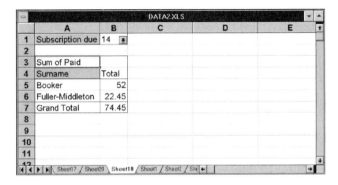

The pivot table has isolated those values whose
[Subscription due] value is [14], and displays:

- The [Surname] and [Paid] data for these
- A revised Grand Total

Experiment with the Pivot Table Wizard to see what
can be achieved.

Updating pivot tables

If you amend the original database on which a pivot
table is based, *Excel 5.0 for Windows* does not
automatically update the relevant values in the table.
However, you can do this manually as often as
necessary. From within the sheet which contains the
pivot table, pull down the [Data] menu and choose
[Refresh Data].

Using the Query and Pivot toolbar

Unless you've hidden it at some time in the past, *Excel 5.0 for Windows* displays the [Query and Pivot] toolbar as soon as you finished defining a pivot table with the Pivot Table Wizard.

**Query &
Pivot
toolbar**

Alternatively, you can launch the [Query and Pivot] toolbar independently by pulling down the [View] menu and choosing [Toolbars]. In the [Toolbars] section of the [Toolbars] dialogue, click on [Query and Pivot] and choose [OK].

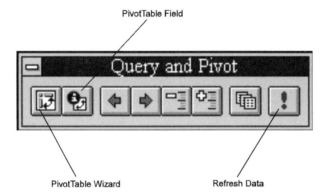

Use the toolbar to initiate a variety of actions. For instance, click on the:

- PivotTable Wizard button to launch the Wizard itself.
- PivotTable Field button to launch the [PivotTable Field] dialogue.
- Refresh Data button to update pivot table data in accordance with changes made to the original database.

Miscellaneous topics

Find file

Excel 5.0 for Windows provides a comprehensive utility for locating files: Find File. You can use Find File with a variety of search criteria: for instance, file contents, date parameters and specific summary information. You can also use Find File to inspect a preview of a file, obtain a directory view or see a file summary.

Running find file

Pull down the [File] menu and choose [Find File].

You can also run Find File from within the [Open] dialogue. Launch the [Open] dialogue by pressing [Ctrl]-[O]. Then click on the [Find File] button.

If this is the first time you've run Find File, the [Search] dialogue launches (if it isn't, you get a variant of the [Find File] dialogue).

The first step in using Find File is to tell *Excel* which directory you want it to look in. If you know the directory details, type them in to the [Location] field.

Directory statement

If you don't know the full directory details and want *Excel* to search through a directory in its entirety, click on the arrow to the right of the [Location] box and click on the drive.

If you don't know the full directory details and want to specify one directory (with or without associated sub-directories), click on the [Advanced Search] button. The [Advanced Search] dialogue launches.

If the [Location] tab isn't already active, click on it. Use the [Directories] field (together with the [Drive] field, if necessary) to locate the directory you want to include in the search. When you've found it, highlight it and click on the [Add] button; *Excel* transfers it to the [Search In] box.

 If you want to include sub-directories in the search, click on [Include Subdirectories].

Choose [OK]. *Excel* inserts the specified directory in the [Location] field in the [Search] dialogue.

In the [Search] dialogue, click in the [File Name] field to specify the file type you want *Excel* to search for (by default, it looks for any *Excel* files). For example, if you want to find any *Excel* files which begin with ACCOUNT, type in **ACCOUNT*.***. Click on [OK] to start the search.

 You can save defined search parameters for future use. Click on the [Save Search As] button. In the [Save Search As] dialogue, type in a name in the [Search Name] field.

Search parameters

Excel launches the [Find File] dialogue.

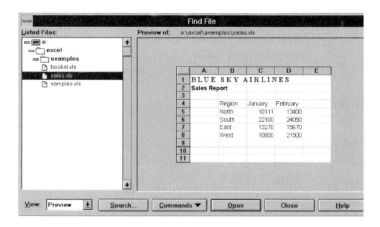

The directory you specified is listed in the [Listed Files] section, together with any files Find File has located. If any files have been found, the first is highlighted. Because [Preview] is selected in the [View] box, *Excel* provides a preview of the highlighted file. If you want to see details of the files, click on the arrow to the right of [View] and choose [File Info] from the list.

If you want to see the associated file summary, click on [Summary].

Opening files

You can open files directly from within the [Find File] dialogue. Highlight the file you want to open in the [Listed Files] dialogue and choose [Open].

You can open multiple files. Hold down [Ctrl] as you click on each file; *Excel* highlights each. Choose [Open] to have each file opened consecutively.

Advanced searches

We've already dealt with the use of the [Advanced Search] dialogue to specify search directories (see 'Directory Statement' earlier). You can also use it to limit a search to specific file contents or summaries, or to precise date ranges (i.e. when files were last saved and created).

Searching for specific file contents/summaries

Launch the [Advanced Search] dialogue by clicking on [Advanced Search] in the [Search] dialogue. If the [Summary] tab isn't already active, click on it.

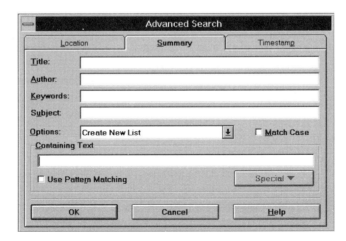

If you want to search for files with specific summary information, enter the information in the relevant fields:

- [Title]
- [Author]
- [Keyword]
- [Subject]

If you want to search for text within files, click in the [Containing Text] field and type in the relevant text string.

Searching for date references

If the [Timestamp] tab isn't already active, click on it. To search for files which were saved within specific date ranges, enter the start and end dates in the [From] and [To] fields in the [Last Saved] section. To search for files which were created within specific date ranges, enter the start and end dates in the [From] and [To] fields in the [Created] section.

[By] field

If you want, you can include the name of the person who last saved or created a file as part of the search criteria. To do this, click in the [By] field in either section within the [Timestamp] tab and type in the name.

When you've finished with the [Advanced Search] dialogue, click on [OK]. *Excel* returns you to the [Search] dialogue. Make any necessary adjustments to this, and click on [OK] to initiate the search. When it locates the specified file(s), *Excel* displays them in the [Find File] dialogue (for how to use this, see 'Running Find File' earlier).

TextWizard

We discussed how to open *Excel* workbooks in 'Opening Existing Workbooks' in Chapter 3. However, *Excel* will readily import a variety of external spreadsheet and database formats. Here's how to do this.

Produce the [Open] dialogue by pressing [Ctrl]-[O]. Click on the arrow to the right of the [List Files of Type] dialogue. In the drop-down list, select the relevant external format. Use the [Directories] field to locate the correct directory; *Excel* displays files which match the format in the [File Name] list. Double-click on the file you want to import to open it into its own format.

Although *Excel* will happily convert numerous third-party formats without any help, there is one kind of file which presents more of a problem. If you try to open Text files, *Excel* launches the TextWizard. The TextWizard is a series of three interactive dialogues which lead you through the steps required to import the contents of Text files across columns.

Text files

In this context, Text files are data lists where varying characters can be used to separate the fields into columns. Because different characters (they're called 'delimiters') can be used to differentiate between fields, *Excel* needs to be told which is being used in a given Text file.

There are other areas *Excel* needs help with. For instance, some Text files are 'fixed width'. This means that each column has a set number of characters.

When you attempt to open a Text file, choose [Text Files (*.prn, *.txt, *.csv)] in the [List Files of Type] section of the [Open] dialogue. *Excel* launches step 1 of TextWizard.

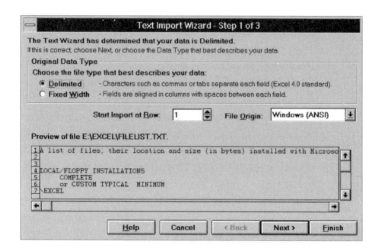

Excel 5.0 for Windows usually detects whether the
Text file is 'Delimited' or 'Fixed Width' and selects the
appropriate option in the [Original Data Type] section.
It also provides a preview of the file in a special section
at the base of the dialogue (use the scroll bars to move
through it if you need to). Amend Step 1 if necessary;
click on [Next] when you've finished. Step 2 launches.

If you chose [Delimited] in Step 1, use Step 2 to specify
the correct delimiters (any changes you make are
reflected in the [Preview] section).

If you selected [Fixed Width] in Step 1, the preview box
shows the suggested placement for column breaks.
Readjust them if necessary by dragging the break
lines.

Click on [Next]. The final TextWizard step launches.
Again, *Excel* normally pre-selects the correct option
here: [General] in the [Column Data Format] section
will import most Text files faithfully. However, some
files require a different approach. Choose [Text] if you
require identification numbers to be treated as text,
[Date] if you want the Text file data treated exclusively
as dates. Choose [Finish] when you have completed

Step 3. *Excel* imports the Text file into an *Excel* database.

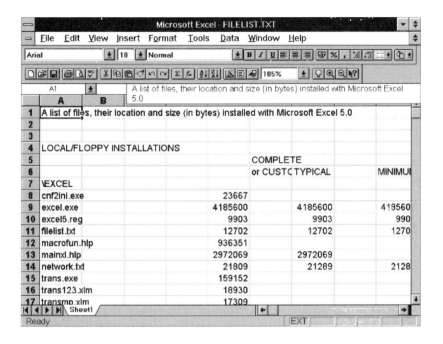

Index

A

Alignment 95, 97
Arguments 154
Arrays 156
   Array formulae............................ 156, 184
      Editing Array formulae................ 159
   Interpolation 158
AutoFill 71, 160
AutoFit 56
AutoOutline 118

B

Backing up 4
Border tab 100

C

Cell ranges 38
   Deleting cell ranges................................ 75
   Selecting cell ranges 80
      Selecting large ranges 82
      Selecting non-adjacent ranges 80
      Selecting ranges on more than
      one worksheet 82
Cells 38
   Clearing cells 73
   Deleting cells 75
   Deleting contents 74
   Editing cells 51
   Entering information 50
   Formatting cells 95
   Moving to specific cells......................... 48
   Selecting cells 80
      Selecting empty cells 86
      Selecting multiple cells 99
      Selecting specific cell types 85
Chart toolbar 218

Charts 208
   Additional data series 215
   AutoFormat 218
   Axes 215
   Creating a separate chart sheet............ 212
   Creating charts 10
   Data labels 214
   Editing a chart 213
   Formatting a chart 213, 216
   Gridlines 215
   Legends 215
   Pictures 215
   Printing 218
   Titles 214
ChartWizard 8, 208
Clearing cells 73
Clipboard 78, 207
Colour 62, 94, 232
Columns 38
   Column width...................................... 55
      Default column width 57
   Column Differences............................... 87
   Deleting columns 76
   Increasing column width 55
   Inserting columns 76
   Inserting sub-headings.......................... 60
   Selecting columns................................ 82
   Selecting multiple columns 83
Comma style button 92
Comparison operators............................ 189
Constants, selecting 86
Currency button.................................... 92
Current Array, selecting......................... 87
Current Region, selecting 87

D

Data Form 186
Databases (lists)................................... 184
Date format 164

Decimal buttons (increasing & decreasing) ..92
Dependents 86
Dialogues 26

E

Edit Mode 51
External references 167
Extrapolation 166

F

Fields 185
    Field names.....................................186
Fill command 71
Fill handle 164
Find 236
Find File 259
    Advanced searches.............................261
    Opening files.....................................261
    Saving search parameters....................260
    Searching for date references 262
    Searching for specific file
    contents/summaries 261
Font tab 98
Format Painter.....................................11, 77
Formula Bar 39, 50, 68
Formulas 67, 232
Function Wizard 152, 156
Functions 151
    Errors 155

G

General tab 233
Go To command.....................................49
Graphics 203
    Clipboard.......................................207
    Filters 7
    Formatting pictures 206
    Inserting images.............................203
    Moving images...............................205
    Patterns tab 206

Resizing images 205
Selecting graphics..............................88
Gridlines 102, 232
    Colouring gridlines 103
Grouping 119
GUI (Graphical User Interface)....................15

H

Header/Footer tab....................................143
Headers/Footers......................................143
    Margins 143
    Customising headers/footers..............144
    Formatting text 145
    Preset headers/footers 144
Hiding 124
    Cell formulae...................................124
    Columns..................................126, 128
    Rows 126
    Workbooks 130
    Worksheets 129

I

Icons 16
Info Window 234
    Printing 235
    Tiling 235
Installation 3
    Complete/Custom 6
    Laptop 6
    Typical 6
Intellisense 8
Interpolation 158

L

Large numbers 53
Last Cell, selecting 88
Launching *Excel 5.0* automatically...............32
Links 167
    Linking data in the same workbook 168
    Linking separate workbooks 169

Updating worksheet links 170
Lists (databases) 184

M

Margins 138
Margins tab 143
Mathematical operators 69
Menu bar 26

N

Name box 40
Naming cells 111
   Deleting names 114
   Names in formulae 114
   Pasting names into the Formula Bar 113
   Permissible names 112
   Substituting names in formulae 112
   Using names 115
New features in *Excel 5.0* 8
Normal style 177
Notes 122
   Copying notes 124
   Deleting notes 123
   Editing notes 123
   Selecting notes 86
Number formats 91
   Custom number formats 92

O

OLE links 11, 207
Operator precedence 69
Outlining 101, 115
   Displaying levels 118
   Removing the outline 120

P

Page breaks 231
Page margins 143

Page numbering 142
Page order 148
Page setup dialogue 138
Page tab 141
Paper size 142
Parentheses 70
Patterns tab 206
Percent button 92
Pivot table wizard 10
Pivot Tables 10, 251
   Query and Pivot toolbar 258
   Setting up a Pivot Table 252
   Updating Pivot Tables 257
Precedents 86
Preferences 230
   Defaults 233
     File location 234
     Font and size 233
     No. of sheets in new workbooks ... 233
     Reference style 233
     Summary info 233
   Formulas 232
   Gridlines 232
   Info window 231
   Note indicator 231
   Page breaks 231
   Row and column headings 232
   Scroll bars 232
   Scrolling 231
   Sheet tabs 232
   Zero values 232
Preview Picture command 203
Print dialogue 138
Print orientation 142
Print quality 142
Printing 135, 140
   Multiple copies 140
   Page ranges 141
   Page setup 141
     Header/Footer tab 143
       Customising headers/footers 144
       Formatting text 145
       Preset headers/footers 144
     Margins tab 143
       Header/Footer margins 143
       Page margins 143

Page positioning 143
Page tab 141
Options 143
Page numbering 142
Paper size............................142
Print orientation 142
Print quality..........................142
Scaling 142
Sheet tab 146
Options 148
Page order............................148
Print area............................146
Print titles............................147
Print preview 135
Margins....................................138
Next and Previous 136
Page Setup dialogue....................138
Print dialogue..............................138
Zoom......................................136
Reports 249
Product Identification Number 5
Protecting a worksheet 125

Query and Pivot toolbar 258

RAM 3
Range address 39
Ranges of cells 38, 78
Records 185
Adding records 188
Deleting records 188
Editing records 187
Restoring records 188
Repeat 120
Replace 236
Reports 241
Printing reports 249
Rounding numbers 53
Row Differences, selecting...........................87
Rows 38

Deleting rows 76
Inserting rows..76
Selecting rows..81
Selecting multiple rows 83

Scaling 142
Scenarios 243
Scenario Manager 243
Defining a scenario.............................244
Inspecting scenarios...........................247
Scenario summaries...........................247
Scroll bars 25, 49, 232
Scroll box 25
Scrolling 231
Searches 189, 236
Case-matching 237
Comparison operators.........................189
Criteria 190
Filtering................................191
AutoFilter 194
Copying filtered records 192
Removing a filter 194
Wild cards 189
Select All button 41
Selecting objects 79
Short-cuts 82
Series 160
Date series....................................164
Extrapolation 166
Linear series 163
Sheet tab 41, 232, 146
Short-cut menus...33
Sorting 197
Columnar data....................................200
Database header rows.........................198
Options button....................................199
Spell checking...103
Starting *Excel* 81
Style button 178
Styles 92, 175
Applying styles....................................176
Copying styles to another workbook....179
Creating styles....................................177

Editing styles 176
Normal style 177
Sum function 68

T

Text files 263
Delimiters...263
Fixed width text files...........................263
Text wrap 97
TextWizard 9, 262
Tip of the Day..230
TipWizard 9, 228
Title bar 25
Toolbars 10, 19, 33, 223
Adding buttons....................................225
Creating your own toolbars 227
Moving toolbars...................................224
Re-sizing toolbars 225
Removing buttons 227

U

Undo 120

V

View Manager..241
Creating a view....................................242
Deleting views.....................................243
Displaying views 243
View tab 230
Visible Cells, selecting 88

W

What-if tables 179, 243
Projections with two variables 182
Wild cards 189
Windows 15
Closing windows...................................20
Horizontal and vertical windows 22

Maximising windows 17
Minimising windows 17
Moving windows...................................19
Moving between windows 22
Re-sizing windows 23
Splitting windows.........................22, 116
Tiling & Cascading windows.................21
Zooming windows 17
Wizards 8, 152, 250
Workbooks 9, 35
Adding more sheets 42
Creating a workbook 36
Opening a workbook 36
Worksheets 37, 111
Creating a new worksheet...............47, 57
Deleting worksheet elements 73
Editing a worksheet 67
Grouping worksheets 84
Inserting new worksheets 37
Selecting worksheets...........................83
Workspaces 106
Automatic workspace loading..............108
Opening workspaces 107
Saving workspace files 107

Other titles from Future Publishing

Copies of the following books are available direct from Future Publishing Limited, Freepost (BS4900) Somerton, Somerset, TA11 6BR. Alternatively they are available in all good bookshops. Retailers can order copies from our distributors, Computer Bookshops, on 021 706 1250

All you need to know imprint

The overall aim of the imprint is to cover the software features most users use most of the time, enabling the reader to get up and running as quickly as possible.

The books assume a familiarity with the Windows environment, and all are written with a series of helpful icons highlighting important information. They are written with a walk-through tutorial style, and make extensive use of illustrations and screen grabs.

All books will be suitable for Beginners and Intermediate users

All you need to know about PCs
by **Geoff Oakshott**
ISBN **1-85870-055-8**
Size 220mm(H) x 150mm(W)
Pages 350
Price **£14.95**
Publication Date **November 1994**
Order no: **FBB0558**

The first book of the 'All you need to know' imprint, serves as an introduction to PCs and also includes 'hints and tips' suitable for the more experienced user. Includes an introduction to computing – the hardware and software, windows and DOS operating systems. If you haven't bought your PC yet this book tells you what you're in for. If you have it'll make it work for you.

All you Need to Know about WordPerfect for Windows (versions 6.0 & 6.1)
by **Stephen Copestake**
ISBN **1-85870-056-6**
Size 220mm(H) x 150mm(W)
Pages 320
Price **£12.95**
Publication Date **November 1994**
Order no: **FBB0566**

Covers version 6.0 with the added refinements included in the latest release 6.1. As well as providing a complete insight into WordPerfect for Windows, the book provides a quick check list of all the new features for those upgrading from previous versions.

All you Need to Know about Lotus 1-2-3 (versions 4.0 & 5.0) for Windows
by **Ian Sinclair**
ISBN **1-85870-058-2**
Size 220mm(H) x 150mm(W)
Pages 300
Price **£12.95**
Publication Date **November 1994**
Order no: **FBB 0582**

The book covers all the main elements of this leading spreadsheet package including its often unexploited data handling capabilities. In order to keep you up to date with all the latest developments the book includes all the refinements of the latest release, version 5.0.

All you Need to Know about CD-ROM
by **Damien Noonan**
ISBN **1-85870-059-0**
Dimensions 230mm(H) x 185mm(W)
Pages 350
Price **£14.95**
Publication Date **November 1994**
Order no: **FBB 0590**

From the publishers of CD-ROM Today magazine, written by the launch editor, Damien Noonan. CD ROM has finally emerged as the way forward for computing, this book provides a comprehensive insight into the technology and its applications.

All you Need to Know about the INTERNET
by **Davey Winder**
ISBN **1-85870-064-7**
Size 230mm(H) x 185mm(W)
Pages 350
Price **£14.95**
Publication Date **November 1994**
Order no: **FBB0647**

A comprehensive guide to exploring the network written by the UK's leading communications expert Davey Winder. Whether you are a beginner or one of the original netsurfers this book will unlock the 'information super-highway'.

Money Management imprint

Money Management with Quicken 6.0 for DOS
by **Jean Miles**
ISBN **1-85870-012-4**
Size 205mm x 120mm
Pages 230
Price **£8.95**
Publication Date **May 1994**
Order no: **FBB0124**

Now into its third print run the book has enjoyed success exceeded only by the software sales!! and is every bit a best seller. It serves as a comprehensive guide to all the facilities of Intuit's DOS version of this leading finance package.

Money Management with Quicken 3.0 for Windows
by **Jean Miles**
ISBN **1-85870-017-5**
Size 220mm x 150mm
Pages 280
Price **£12.95**
Publication Date **April 1994**
Order no: **FBB0175**

The second Quicken book from the pen of Jean Miles, this book has the Official backing of the software publishers, Intuit Software. A comprehensive look at this latest release of Quicken. This book is already established on the path to best seller status.

Money Management with Sage Moneywise 2.0 for Windows
by **Jean Miles**
ISBN **1-85870-043-4**
Size 220mm x 150mm
Pages 250
Price **£12.95**
Publication Date **October 1994**
Order no: **FBB0434**

The third Money Management book from Jean Miles. Covers all the features of SageSoft's entry level package Moneywise. As with all the Money Management books it has the full endorsement of the software developers Sage.

Money Management with Microsoft Money 3.0 for Windows
by **Andrew Marlow**
ISBN **1-85870-044-2**
Size 220mm x 150mm
Pages 280
Price **£12.95**
Publication Date **October 1994**
Order no: **FB 0442**

The fourth book of the imprint, written for Microsoft's latest version of their personal accounting package, Money 3.0.

Professional imprint

The Complete Desktop Publishing Guidebook
by **Simon Williams & Geoffrey Oakshott**
ISBN **1-85870-003-5**
Size 235mm x 185mm
Pages 470
Price **£24.95**
Publication Date **October 1994**
Order no: **FBB0035**

A thorough insight into desktop publishing and design. This book provides all the advise and guidance on how to use dtp as an effective business tool. From the Publishers of PC Plus magazine.

Successful Business Accounting with Sage Sterling +2 Version 2
by **Andrew Marlow**
ISBN **1-85870-013-2**
Size 235mm x 185mm
Pages 300
Price **£24.95**
Publication Date **June 1994**
Order no: **FBB0132**

A comprehensive look at the Sage +2 range of business products, comes complete with a free, complete copy of the Bank Interest Calculator software direct from Sage UK, with a number of business templates produced by the Author. Another officially endorsed books from Future Publishing.

The Complete Access Workbook
by **Arthur Tennick**
ISBN **1-85870-011-6**
Size 223mm x 190mm
Pages 250
Price **£17.95**
Publication Date **May 1994**
Order no: **FBB0116**

A comprehensive database package requires something similar from a book. The Complete Access Workbook provides something for every type of user whether an absolute beginner or a professional programmer. It will guide you through the process of designing your database.

The Modem and Communications Guidebook
by **Sue Schofield**
ISBN **1-85870-000-0**
Size 235mm x 185mm
Pages 350
Price **£19.95**
Publication Date **November 1993**
Order no: **FBB0000**

Written and researched in the UK, this book makes communications easy to learn, productive and trouble-free. Clear explanations of all the basic ideas without the unnecessary jargon, make the process of going on-line painless and straightforward. This book has very quickly established itself as a best seller. Book includes free comms software and CIX subscription.

Windows 3.1 HelpScreen
by **Arthur Tennick**
ISBN **1-85870-001-9**
Size 223mm x 190mm
Pages 350
Price **£19.95**
Publication **November 1993**
Order no: **FBB0019**

Provides the straight forward answers to all the questions you might have about Windows - this book is for those with a basic familiarity with Windows but who wish to progress and quickly build their expertise. With a wealth of Windows books available it is reassuring to know you have the hallmark of authority from the UK's leading PC magazine PC Plus.

The PC Plus HelpScreen Collection
by **Barry Thomas**
ISBN **1-85870-002-7**
Size 240mm x 205mm
Price **£14.95** (includes disk)
Pages 150
Publication Date **October 1993**
Order no: **FBB0027**

A compilation of the last two years of HelpScreen pages within PC Plus. All material has been edited and rewritten to provide accessible time saving information.

The Software Guide
Size 240mm x170mm
Pages 450
Price **£24.95**
Publication Date **March 1994**
Order no: **PSG003**

The authoritative new directory of IBM-compatible PC software, this book comes to you from the publishers of the Britain's best selling PC magazine, PC Plus. It provides details of more than 3000 software products including hardware requirements, price and feature analysis.

Future Books
Priority Order Form

You can use this tear-off coupon to order any of the Future Publishing books described on the previous pages. Simply fill in the details in the spaces provided and post this coupon (or a photocopy), together with payment, in an envelope to the following address:

Future Book Orders, Future Publishing Ltd, Freepost (BS4900), Somerton, Somerset TA11 6BR

Your name...

Your address ....

....Postcode....................................

Your signature..

Please send me (tick as appropriate):

☐	All you need to know about PCs	FBB0558	£14.95
☐	All you need to know about WordPerfect for Windows (versions 6.0 & 6.1)	FBB0566	£12.95
☐	All you need to know about Excel 5.0 for Windows	FBB0574	£12.95
☐	All you need to know about Lotus 1-2-3 (versions 4.0 & 5.0) for Windows	FBB0582	£12.95
☐	All you need to know about CD-ROM	FBB0590	£14.95
☐	All you need to know about the Internet	FBB0647	£14.95
☐	Money Management with Quicken 6.0 for DOS	FBB0124	£8.95
☐	Money Management with Quicken 3.0 for Windows	FBB0175	£12.95
☐	Money Management with Sage Moneywise 2.0 for Windows	FBB0434	£12.95
☐	Money Management with Microsoft Money 3.0 for Windows	FBB0442	£12.95
☐	The Complete Desktop Publishing Guidebook	FBB0035	£24.95
☐	Successful Business Accounting with Sage Sterling +2 Version 2	FBB0132	£24.95
☐	The Complete Access Workbook	FBB0116	£17.95
☐	The Modem and Communications Guidebook	FBB0000	£19.95
☐	Windows 3.1 Helpscreen	FBB0019	£19.95
☐	The PC Plus Helpscreen Collection	FBB0027	£14.95
☐	The Software Guide	PSG003	£24.95

Amount enclosed   (Make cheques, P/Os etc. payable to Future Publishing Ltd.)

Method of payment (tick one): VISA ☐   ACCESS ☐   CHEQUE ☐   POSTAL ORDER

CARD NUMBER   ☐☐☐☐ ☐☐☐☐ ☐☐☐☐ ☐☐☐☐

EXPIRY DATE   ☐☐ ☐☐

Tick here if you do not wish to receive direct mail from other companies ☐

Now send this coupon (or a photocopy) and your payment to the address on the front of this coupon..
**You will not need a stamp when you post this order and postage and packing are free. There
are no extra costs.** Please allow 28 days for delivery.   **AYNTKEX**